CHRONOLOGY OF BOSTON RED SOX RECORDS

Also by John A. Mercurio

CHRONOLOGY OF MAJOR LEAGUE BASEBALL RECORDS
CHRONOLOGY OF NEW YORK YANKEE RECORDS

CHRONOLOGY OF
BOSTON RED SOX
RECORDS

JOHN A. MERCURIO

HARPER & ROW, PUBLISHERS, NEW YORK

Cambridge, Philadelphia, San Francisco
London, Mexico City, São Paulo, Singapore, Sydney

The photographs on pages 5, 7, 33, 67, 77, 87, and 98 are courtesy of the National Baseball Hall of Fame and Museum, Inc., Cooperstown, N.Y.

CHRONOLOGY OF BOSTON RED SOX RECORDS. Copyright © 1989 by John A. Mercurio. *All rights reserved.* Printed in the United States of America. No part of this book may be used or reproduced in any manner whatsoever without written permission except in the case of brief quotations embodied in critical articles and reviews. For information address Harper & Row, Publishers, Inc., 10 East 53rd Street, New York, N.Y. 10022. Published simultaneously in Canada by Fitzhenry & Whiteside Limited, Toronto.

FIRST EDITION

Designer: Joan Greenfield

LIBRARY OF CONGRESS CATALOG CARD NUMBER: 88-4572
ISBN 0-06-096335-2

89 90 91 92 93   **FG**   10 9 8 7 6 5 4 3 2 1

To Jonathan

CONTENTS

PREFACE

The Boston Red Sox were one of the original teams to begin play in the American League in 1901. In the beginning the team was called the Pilgrims. Sometimes they were called the Boston Americans, and they were not named the Red Sox until owner John I. Taylor made the announcement in 1907.

The club almost won the pennant in their very first year, falling just four games shy while ending up in second place under player-manager Jimmy Collins. After falling back to third place in 1902, Collins brought them home a winner for the first time in 1903. Collins also guided the team to its very first World Series title that year and repeated winning the pennant in 1904. However, he did not have the opportunity to win a second World Series because the two leagues were at war with each other that year.

The Red Sox have had a very exciting history, which has seen and produced such Hall of Famers as Cy Young, Babe Ruth, Harry Hooper, Ted Williams, Bobby Doerr, Jimmy Foxx, Jimmy Collins, Rick Ferrall, Tris Speaker, Joe Cronin, Lefty Grove, Herb Pennock, and Red Ruffing.

This book is about all the great Red Sox players and the marvelous records they have created. Unlike a typical record book, which only presents the existing set of records, this book starts with the first set of records in 1901 and updates them in chronological order so that every record is seen and preserved. A sample of a chronological listing for the Red Sox season home run record would look like this:

Most Home Runs

1901	Buck Freeman	12
1903	Buck Freeman	13
1919	Babe Ruth	29
1936	Jimmy Foxx	41
1938	**Jimmy Foxx**	**50**

The chronological listing shows that Buck Freeman was the club's first home run champion in 1901 and that he broke his own record in 1903. Freeman's record would last 16 years before part-time pitcher and part-time outfielder Babe Ruth astounded the baseball world by pounding 29 round-trippers. The reaction to Babe Ruth's home runs so excited baseball fans that a new, "livelier" ball was introduced in the following year so that fans could further enjoy the wonderful sight of the majestic home run.

But Boston fans would be robbed of seeing Babe Ruth hit any more home runs for them—as history well knows, he was traded the next year to the rival Yankees for $125,000 in cash.

The Red Sox home run record stayed intact for 17 years before Jimmy "The Beast" Foxx would rap 41 balls, many of them over the "Green Monster," Fenway Park's famed left-field wall. Foxx, who also had the nickname of "Double X," was double trouble to enemy pitchers, and in 1939 he blasted 50 balls out of sight to set a Boston home run record that to this date has not been broken.

Thus the chronological list represents a complete history of the home run record, from the start to the existing record holder. This book uses this concept in categories of batting, pitching, and fielding. Season and career records are presented, as well as rookie and manager records.

Another new feature found in this book is players' Record Profiles. It is for the very first time possible to see every record created by every Red Sox player in a complete profile. This book gives this honor to Boston's greatest players.

This book also introduces a new Record Holders List, at the end of each chapter, showing the exact number of records established by each and every Red Sox player. A Composite Record Holders List, near the end of the book, reveals previously unknown information about which Red Sox players and pitchers have the most records.

CHAPTER 1

SEASON BATTING RECORDS

BATTING QUIZ

1. Due to a one-game playoff, he became the only player in baseball history to play in 163 regular-season games in one season. Name him.
2. This present-day Boston star slammed 240 hits to break a Hall of Famer's 73-year-old team record. Who is this modern great and whose record did he break?
3. The all-time Red Sox leader in doubles is not a well-known player. Do you remember him?
4. What Red Sox player belted the most home runs in one season?
5. What Red Sox player erased Babe Ruth's record for the highest home run percentage?

DID YOU KNOW that Ted Williams has five unbroken season batting records?

DID YOU KNOW that Jimmy Foxx had one of the greatest years of any Red Sox player? In 1938 "Double X" blasted 50 home runs, drove in 175 runs, and slugged a staggering .704.

DID YOU KNOW that Tris Speaker established nine marvelous records in one season (1912)?

Most Games

1901	Tommy Dowd	*138
	Jimmy Collins	*138
	Hobe Ferris	*138
	Freddy Parent	*138
1902	Buck Freeman	138
	Freddy Parent	138
1903	Buck Freeman	141
	Hobe Ferris	141
1904	Chick Stahl	157
	Candy LaChance	157
1914	Tris Speaker	158
1961	Chuck Schilling	158
1962	Carl Yastrzemski	160
1966	George Scott	162
1969	Carl Yastrzemski	162
1978	**Jim Rice**	***163

Most At Bats

1901	Tommy Dowd	*594
1904	Pat Dougherty	*647
1924	Bill Wambsganss	636
1936	Doc Cramer	643
1938	Doc Cramer	658
1977	Rick Burleson	663
1978	**Jim Rice**	**677**

Most Hits

1901	Jimmy Collins	187
1903	Pat Dougherty	195
1912	Tris Speaker	222
1985	**Wade Boggs**	**240**

Most Singles

1901	Tommy Dowd	131
1902	Pat Dougherty	132
1903	Pat Dougherty	160
1942	Johnny Pesky	165
1985	**Wade Boggs**	**187**

Most Doubles

1901	Jimmy Collins	42
1912	Tris Speaker	53
1931	**Earl Webb**	***67

Most Triples

1901	Jimmy Collins	16
1902	Buck Freeman	19
1903	Buck Freeman	20
1904	**Chick Stahl**	**22**
1913	**Tris Speaker**	**22**

Most Home Runs

1901	Buck Freeman	12
1903	Buck Freeman	13
1919	Babe Ruth	**29
1936	Jimmy Foxx	41
1938	**Jimmy Foxx**	**50**

Most Grand Slams

| 1919 | Babe Ruth | 4 |

Highest Home Run Percentage

1901	Buck Freeman	2.4
1918	Babe Ruth	*3.5
1919	Babe Ruth	**6.7
1936	Jimmy Foxx	7.0
1938	Jimmy Foxx	8.8
1955	Ted Williams	8.8
1957	**Ted Williams**	**9.0**

Most Extra Base Hits

1901	Jimmy Collins	64
1902	Buck Freeman	68
1903	Buck Freeman	72
1912	Tris Speaker	75
1919	Babe Ruth	75
1931	Earl Webb	84
1938	**Jimmy Foxx**	**92**

Most Total Bases

1901	Jimmy Collins	279
1902	Buck Freeman	283
1912	Tris Speaker	329
1938	Jimmy Foxx	398
1978	**Jim Rice**	**406**

Most Runs

1901	Jimmy Collins	108
1903	Pat Dougherty	108
1912	Tris Speaker	136
1938	Jimmy Foxx	139
1942	Ted Williams	141
1946	Ted Williams	142
1949	**Ted Williams**	**150**

* American League Record
** Major League Record
*** Unbroken Major League Record

Most RBIs
1901	Buck Freeman	114
1902	Buck Freeman	121
1936	Jimmy Foxx	143
1938	**Jimmy Foxx**	**175**

Most Bases on Balls
1901	Chick Stahl	54
1904	Chick Stahl	64
1912	Tris Speaker	82
1915	Harry Hooper	89
1919	Babe Ruth	101
1926	Topper Rigney	108
1938	Jimmy Foxx	119
1941	Ted Williams	145
1942	Ted Williams	145
1946	Ted Williams	156
1947	**Ted Williams**	**162**
1949	**Ted Williams**	**162**

Most Strikeouts
1901–12 Statistics Not Kept
1913	Duffy Lewis	55
1915	Duffy Lewis	63
1931	Urbane Pickering	71
1936	Jimmy Foxx	119
1963	Dick Stuart	144
1966	George Scott	152
1977	**Butch Hobson**	**162**

Most Stolen Bases
1901	Tommy Dowd	33
1903	Pat Dougherty	35
1909	Harry Lord	36
1910	Harry Hooper	40
1912	Tris Speaker	52
1973	**Tommy Harper**	**54**

Highest Batting Average
1901	Buck Freeman	.345
1912	Tris Speaker	.383
1941	**Ted Williams**	**.406**

Highest Slugging Percentage
1901	Buck Freeman	.527
1912	Tris Speaker	.567
1919	Babe Ruth	*.657
1938	Jimmy Foxx	.704
1941	**Ted Williams**	**.735**

Most Pinch At Bats
1901	Ossee Schreckengost	9
1903	Jake Stahl	*11
1904	Duke Farrell	11
1905	Moose Grimshaw	11
1907	John Hoey	18
1911	Jack Thoney	20
1917	Chick Shorten	24
1924	Phil Todt	30
1925	Tex Vache	49
1966	Lenny Green	52
1984	**Rick Miller**	**53**

Most Pinch Hits
1901	Ossee Schrenckengost	3
1903	Jake Stahl	5
1907	John Hoey	8
1925	Tex Vache	10
1929	Ken Williams	10
1935	Bing Miller	13
1943	**Joe Cronin**	**18**

Highest Pinch Batting Average
(Minimum 10 At Bats)
1904	Duke Farrell	.090
1905	Moose Grimshaw	.272
1907	John Hoey	.444
1908	Amby McConnell	.500
1960	**Vic Wertz**	**.555**

Most Sacrifice Bunts
1905	Freddy Parent	35

Most Sacrifice Flies
1955	Jackie Jensen	12
1956	Jimmy Piersall	12
1959	**Jackie Jensen**	**12**

Fewest Strikeouts
(Minimum 500 At Bats)
1921	**Stuffy McInnis**	**9**

Most Hit By Pitch
1986	**Don Baylor**	**35**

DID YOU KNOW that Fenway Park is the last remaining single-deck big-league stadium?

Most Game Winning RBIs

1984	Jim Rice	17

Consecutive Games with RBIs

1939	Joe Cronin	12
1942	Ted Williams	12

Longest Hitting Streak

1902	Buck Freeman	26
1912	Tris Speaker	30
1949	Dom DiMaggio	34

RECORD HOLDERS LIST

1	Buck Freeman	15
2	Ted Williams	13
3	Jimmy Foxx	12
3	Tris Speaker	12
5	Jimmy Collins	7
5	Babe Ruth	7
5	Pat Dougherty	7
8	Tommy Dowd	4
8	Jim Rice	4
8	Chick Stahl	4
11	John Hoey	3
11	Freddy Parent	3
13	Wade Boggs	2
13	Jackie Jensen	2
13	Joe Cronin	2
13	Ossee Schreckengost	2

13	Tex Vache	2
13	Duke Farrell	2
13	Harry Hooper	2
13	Duffy Lewis	2
13	Earl Webb	2
13	Doc Cramer	2
13	George Scott	2
13	Carl Yastrzemski	2
13	Jake Stahl	2
26	Candy LaChance	1
26	Chuck Schilling	1
26	Bill Wambsganss	1
26	Rick Burleson	1
26	Urbane Pickering	1
26	Dick Stuart	1
26	Butch Hobson	1
26	Topper Rigney	1
26	Harry Lord	1
26	Jack Thoney	1
26	Chick Shorten	1
26	Phil Todt	1
26	Jimmy Piersall	1
26	Stuffy McInnis	1
26	Dom DiMaggio	1
26	Lenny Green	1
26	Jack O'Brien	1
26	Bing Miller	1
26	Ken Williams	1
26	Amby McConnell	1
26	Vic Wertz	1
26	Rick Miller	1
26	Don Baylor	1

SUMMARY AND HIGHLIGHTS

The original Red Sox team of 1901 had Buck Freeman on first, Hobe Ferris at second, Freddy Parent at short, Jimmy Collins (their player-manager) at third, Ossee Schreckengost and Lou Criger behind the plate, Tommy Dowd in left, Chick Stahl in center, and Charlie Hemphill in right. On the mound they had Cy Young, Ted Lewis, George Winter, Fred Mitchell, and Nig Cuppy.

Buck Freeman was the first Boston star. The team, which was called the Pilgrims at the time, was made up of many players taken from the National League by American League president Ban Johnson's raiders.

Freeman led the club in batting with a solid .345, smashed 12 home runs to become the club's first home run champion, and drove in 114 runs. He would be the club leader for the next five years and be responsible for 15 of the original records.

TED WILLIAMS

RECORD PROFILE
TED WILLIAMS
SEASON BATTING RECORDS

1941	Most Bases on Balls	145	1 year before tied
	Highest Batting Average	.406	**NEVER BROKEN**
	Highest Slugging Percentage	.735	**NEVER BROKEN**
1942	Most Runs	141	4 years before broken
	Most Consecutive RBI Games	12	**NEVER BROKEN**
	Most Bases on Balls	145	4 years before broken
1946	Most Bases on Balls	156	1 year before broken
	Most Runs	142	3 years before broken
1947	Most Bases on Balls	162	1 year before tied
1949	Most Bases on Balls	162	**NEVER BROKEN**
	Most Runs	150	**NEVER BROKEN**
1955	Home Run Percentage	8.8	2 years before broken
1957	Home Run Percentage	9.0	**NEVER BROKEN**

The Red Sox were blessed with many outstanding players in the years that followed, and they would have been one of the greatest teams in baseball if it weren't for their "part-time" owner, Harry Frazee. Frazee was more interested in the production of his Broadway plays than in his baseball team, and each time one of his plays was a failure, he would need great sums of money to pay his debts. In order to survive, Frazee would sell off his best baseball players. The most famous deal was Babe Ruth to the Yankees in 1920. Frazee received $125,000, plus a $300,000 loan that would go toward financing more of his plays.

In 1916 Tris Speaker was traded to Cleveland as a result of a contract dispute. In return the Red Sox received Sad Sam Jones, Fred Thomas, and $55,000. Next to the Ruth trade it would be the worst trade in Boston history. But there were many more trades that would follow as Frazee milked the club for every penny he could get. In a five-year period he would trade away 15 players (mostly to the Yankees). When Harry Hooper was sent to Chicago in 1921, Boston had lost a complete Hall of Fame outfield in Speaker, Ruth, and Hooper. In addition, Frazee sold his best pitchers—Carl Mays, Joe Bush, Sam Jones, Waite Hoyt, Herb Pennock, and Red Ruffing (all to the Yankees). All of these pitchers were at one time 20-game winners, and Hoyt, Pennock, and Ruffing became Hall of Famers! When Wally Schang, a top-notch catcher, Everett Scott, the league's best-fielding shortstop, and Joe Dugan, a fine third baseman, were also sold to the Yankees, the dismantling of the Red Sox was complete. All of these players contributed to the Yankee dynasty.

As a result of Frazee's famous sales, the Red Sox finished last nine of the next 12 seasons, with two next-to-last-place finishes. Prior to that, the club was world champion in 1915, 1916, and 1918. They would not again be competitive until the arrival of their greatest player, Ted Williams, in 1939. But the Yankees had become so powerful that Boston would not win another pennant until 1946.

Ted Williams would soon be called the "Splendid Splinter," for at 6'4" and 225 pounds he was to become one of the game's greatest sluggers. Williams also acquired another nickname, the "Thumper," and he accumulated 13 marvelous season records, of which seven are still unbroken today.

Williams did extremely well in his rookie season of 1939. The Rookie of the Year Award had not yet been thought of, but Ted would have won it hands down. In his sensational rookie season he slammed 31 home runs, scored 131 runs, drove in a Major League rookie record 145 runs, batted .327, and slugged .609. He continued to do well his second year by crunching 193 hits and batting .344, but it would be his third year that would make him famous.

The Splendid Splinter went into the last day of the season with exactly a .400 batting average. A home doubleheader was to be played, but the games were unimportant because the Yankees had already wrapped up the pen-

TRIS SPEAKER

RECORD PROFILE
TRIS SPEAKER
SEASON BATTING RECORDS

1912	Most Hits	222	73 years before broken
	Most Doubles	53	19 years before broken
	Most Extra Base Hits	75	19 years before broken
	Most Total Bases	329	27 years before broken
	Most Runs	136	26 years before broken
	Highest Batting Average	.383	29 years before broken
	Highest Slugging Percentage	.567	7 years before broken
	Most Bases on Balls	82	3 years before broken
	Most Stolen Bases	52	61 years before broken
1913	Most Triples	22	**NEVER BROKEN**
1914	Most Games	158	48 years before broken

nant. Manager Joe Cronin had asked Williams if he wanted to sit out to preserve his .400 batting average. If he chose not to play, the fans who had filled the park to see him would accuse him of not having courage. More important, Williams would accuse himself of being a coward and then would have to live with that the rest of his life. So he picked up a few bats and began his long-legged stride onto the field.

The fans roared their approval as he entered the batter's box. The Red Sox were playing Connie Mack and his Athletics, and As' catcher Ted Hayes wished Williams the best of luck and told him that Connie Mack would make him earn his .400 batting average. The Thumper accepted the challenge and promptly slashed a single and home run in his first two at bats, and then added two more singles. Cronin then wanted Ted to sit out the second game, but again the Boston slugger wanted to play. He was determined to see the thing through to the end. After getting two more hits, Williams ended the season with a .406 average, and no player has batted .400 since. Williams would have even more records if he hadn't spent 5 years in the Army. Including his first three seasons, Ted Williams would bat over .300 for 17 years in a row. It wouldn't be until 1959 that Ted would suffer a poor season, and that was the next-to-last year of his career. But he recovered to bring his average above .300 in 1960, his final hour.

Ted Williams was not the first Red Sox superstar. That honor goes to Tris Speaker. Many have said that Joe DiMaggio, Willie Mays, Mickey Mantle, and Duke Snider cannot match the accomplishments of Tris Speaker in center field. In addition to being an exceptional fielder, "The Spoke," as he was called, had tremendous seasons, batting .340, .327, .383, .365, and .338 before he was traded to Cleveland. And when Speaker got to Cleveland, he continued batting—.386, .352, .318, .296, .388, .362, .378, .380, .344, .389, .304, and .327—before retiring with a final-season batting average of .267. The players received in the trade, Sam Jones and Fred Thomas, did very little for the Red Sox.

Before Speaker left the New England area, he left his name in the record book 12 times and was the first Bostonian to bang out 200 hits in one season. In 1912 he hit safely 222 times, an achievement that would remain unsurpassed for 73 years before present-day star Wade Boggs eclipsed it.

Even though Speaker played most of his career in the dead-ball era, he was not a singles hitter. He was first on the team to belt more than 50 doubles in a season, and his 22 triples is a record that only Chick Stahl has tied. In his fabulous career Tris Speaker would stroke more doubles than any player in baseball history!

Part of his ability to rack up the most doubles was the fact that he possessed blazing speed, which also enabled him to swipe 52 bases in 1912, a team record that would stand 61 years before Tommy Harper would be successful 54 times.

Another superstar was Jimmy "The Beast" Foxx. Also known as "Double X," he was double trouble any time he walked up to the plate. When asked

JIMMY FOXX

RECORD PROFILE
JIMMY FOXX
SEASON BATTING RECORDS

1936	Most Home Runs	41	2 years before broken
	Highest Home Run Percentage	7.0	2 years before broken
	Most RBIs	143	2 years before broken
	Most Strikeouts	119	27 years before broken
1938	Most Home Runs	50	**NEVER BROKEN**
	Highest Home Run Percentage	8.8	19 years before broken
	Most Runs	139	4 years before broken
	Most RBIs	175	**NEVER BROKEN**
	Highest Slugging Percentage	.704	3 years before broken
	Most Bases on Balls	119	3 years before broken
	Most Extra Base Hits	92	**NEVER BROKEN**
	Most Total Bases	398	40 years before broken

how he wanted to pitch to Foxx, Lefty Grove said, "I'd rather not throw the ball at all."

Foxx registered 12 fine marks, and three of them have never been broken. His most outstanding season was in 1938, when he batted .349 and became the first Boston player to slug over .700. His 50 home runs are the most of any Red Sox player. In this spectacular year the Beast drove in 175 runs, and even the great Ted Williams could not match or better Foxx's home run or RBI records. It should be noted that Foxx did not come to the Red Sox until 1936, when he was already past his prime in a career that began in 1925. Nevertheless the rugged 195-pounder had home run seasons of 41, 36, 50, 35, 36, and 19 before moving on to the Cubs in 1942.

Earl Webb had a very unusual year (for him) in 1931, when he blasted 67 doubles, which represents a Major League record that still stands. The most doubles Webb had hit before was 30, and he never came close to doing it again.

Present-day stars Jim Rice and Wade Boggs are keeping the Red Sox fans' hopes high as they continue to play well. Rice created an unusual record in 1978, when he appeared in 163 games in one season. It was the year that the Red Sox lost a one-game playoff to the Yankees, and Rice had played in all 162 games of the season. Others had played in 162 games, but Jim Rice is the only player in history to make it 163.

Wade Boggs, who is presently battling Don Mattingly of the Yankees for the honor of being considered the game's best hitter, cracked 240 hits in 1985 to break Tris Speaker's record set in 1912. Boggs is well on his way to becoming the next Boston superstar.

CHAPTER II

SEASON PITCHING RECORDS

PITCHING QUIZ

1. Two Red Sox pitchers have won more than 30 games in one season. Name them.
2. This outstanding pitcher once lost 25 games for the Red Sox in one season, but he still made the Hall of Fame. Name him.
3. Can you name the Red Sox starting pitcher who has the highest winning percentage?
4. The lowest ERA ever turned in by a Boston pitcher is 1.01. This is also an unbroken Major League record. Can you name this pitcher?
5. The Red Sox strikeout record was 258 and was set 76 years ago. Do you know who recently broke this mark with 291?

DID YOU KNOW that in 1901 Cy Young started 41 games, completed 38, and won 33?

DID YOU KNOW that in 1912 Joe Wood won 34 games and lost only five? His winning percentage was an astronomical .872, and his ERA was a cool 1.91.

DID YOU KNOW that in 1964 Dick Radatz had the greatest year of any Red Sox relief pitcher? The "Monster" appeared in 79 games, won 16, lost nine, and saved 29.

Most Appearances

1901	Cy Young	43
1902	Cy Young	45
1909	Frank Arellanes	45
1916	Dutch Leonard	48
1939	Emerson Dickman	48
1950	Ellis Kinder	48
1951	Ellis Kinder	63
1953	Ellis Kinder	*69
1960	Mike Fornieles	70
1964	**Dick Radatz**	**79**

Most Starts

1901	Cy Young	41
1902	**Cy Young**	***43**

Most Complete Games

1901	Cy Young	38
1902	**Cy Young**	***41**

Most Wins

1901	Cy Young	*33
1912	**Joe Wood**	**34**

Most Losses

1901	Ted Lewis	17
1902	Bill Dinneen	21
1906	Bill Dinneen	21
	Joe Harris	21
1927	Slim Harriss	21
1928	**Red Ruffing**	**25**

Highest Winning Percentage

1901	Cy Young	.767
1912	**Joe Wood**	***.872**

Lowest ERA

1901	Cy Young	*1.62
1914	**Dutch Leonard**	****1.01**

Most Innings

1901	Cy Young	371
1902	**Cy Young**	***386**

Most Hits Allowed

1901	Cy Young	324
1902	**Cy Young**	**337**

Most Bases on Balls

1901	Ted Lewis	91
1902	Bill Dinneen	99
1906	Joe Harris	99
1916	Babe Ruth	118
1923	Howard Ehmke	119
1936	Wes Ferrell	119
1937	Jack Wilson	119
1949	**Mel Parnell**	**134**

Most Strikeouts

1901	Cy Young	*158
1902	Cy Young	166
1903	Cy Young	183
1904	Cy Young	203
1905	Cy Young	208
1911	Joe Wood	231
1912	Joe Wood	258
1988	**Roger Clemens**	**291**

Most Shutouts

1901	Cy Young	*5
1903	Cy Young	*7
1904	**Cy Young**	***10**
1912	**Joe Wood**	**10**

Longest Winning Streak

1912	Joe Wood	16

DID YOU KNOW that Babe Ruth used to tip off his curve by sticking out his tongue?

DID YOU KNOW that Howard Ehmke was credited with a no-hitter because opposing pitcher Slim Harriss failed to touch first base after hitting a double? Ehmke was then denied a second consecutive no-hitter when the official ruled a booted ball by his third baseman a hit.

* American League Record
** Major League Record
*** Unbroken Major League Record

Longest Losing Streak

1906	Joe Harris	14

Most Hit Batsmen

1923	Howard Ehmke	20

Most Wild Pitches

1963	Earl Wilson	21

RELIEF PITCHING RECORDS

Most Games

1901	Ted Lewis	5
1903	George Winter	6
1905	George Winter	8
1906	Ralph Glaze	9
1907	Tex Pruiett	18
1910	Charley Hall	19
1911	Charley Hall	22
1913	Charley Hall	31
1915	Carl Mays	32
1926	Tony Welzer	34
1931	Wilcy Moore	38
1933	Johnny Welch	40
1939	Emerson Dickman	47
1943	Mace Brown	49
1951	Ellis Kinder	61
1953	Ellis Kinder	*69
1960	Mike Fornieles	70
1964	**Dick Radatz**	**79**

Most Wins

1901	Cy Young	2
1903	Cy Young	2
1904	Cy Young	2
	Jesse Tannehill	2
1905	Cy Young	5
1910	Charley Hall	6
	Joe Wood	6
1911	Joe Wood	6
1912	Charley Hall	6
	Hugh Bedient	6
1916	Carl Mays	6
1931	Wilcy Moore	7
1939	Joe Heving	11
1956	Ike Delock	11
1963	Dick Radatz	*15
1964	**Dick Radatz**	***16**

Most Losses

1901	Ted Lewis	2
1903	George Winter	2
1907	Ralph Glaze	2
1908	Tex Pruiett	2
	Ed Cicotte	2
1910	Joe Wood	3
1911	Charley Hall	3
1913	Dutch Leonard	5
1914	Hugh Bedient	5
1920	Benn Karr	6
1932	Wilcy Moore	8
1954	Ellis Kinder	8
1964	Dick Radatz	9
1965	Dick Radatz	*11
1976	**Jim Willoughby**	**12**

Most Wins Plus Saves

1901	Cy Young	2
1903	Cy Young	4
1905	Cy Young	5
1909	Frank Arellanes	**11
1915	Carl Mays	12
1931	Wilcy Moore	17
1939	Joe Heving	18
1951	Ellis Kinder	24
1953	Ellis Kinder	37
1963	Dick Radatz	40
1964	**Dick Radatz**	****45**

Most Saves

1901	Ted Lewis	1
1903	Cy Young	2
	Bill Dinneen	2
1906	Cy Young	2
1907	Cy Young	3
	Tex Pruiett	3
1909	Frank Arellanes	**8
1931	Wilcy Moore	10
1951	Ellis Kinder	14
1953	Ellis Kinder	**27
1964	Dick Radatz	**29
1977	Bill Campbell	31
1983	**Bob Stanley**	**33**

Lefty Gomez on how to pitch to Jimmy Foxx: "I'd rather not throw the ball at all."

Highest Winning Percentage
(Minimum 10 Decisions)

1939	Joe Heving (11–2)	.846
1951	**Ellis Kinder (10–1)**	**.909**

Lowest ERA
(Minimum 25 Games)

1913	Charley Hall	3.43
1915	Carl Mays	2.60
1943	Mace Brown	2.12
1953	Ellis Kinder	1.85
1986	**Calvin Schiraldi**	**1.41**

Most Innings

1913	Charley Hall	63
1915	Carl Mays	78
1926	Tony Welzer	96
1939	Emerson Dickman	102
1951	Ellis Kinder	107
1953	Ellis Kinder	107
1960	Mike Fornieles	109
1963	Jack Lamabe	139
1964	Dick Radatz	157
1982	**Bob Stanley**	**168**

Most Hits Allowed

1913	Charley Hall	93
1926	Tony Welzer	105
1931	Wilcy Moore	123
1939	Emerson Dickman	126
1941	Mike Ryba	130
1963	Jack Lamabe	131
1982	**Bob Stanley**	**161**

Most Bases on Balls

1913	Charley Hall	30
1926	Tony Welzer	48
1943	Mace Brown	51
1956	Ike Delock	54
1964	Dick Radatz	58
1977	**Bill Campbell**	**60**

Cy Young's response, when asked by a youngster if he had ever pitched in the big leagues: "Son, I've won more games than you'll ever see."

Most Strikeouts

1913	Charley Hall	31
1915	Carl Mays	39
1933	Johnny Welch	47
1951	Ellis Kinder	74
1956	Ike Delock	83
1962	Dick Radatz	144
1963	Dick Radatz	162
1964	**Dick Radatz**	**181**

Chronology of Red Sox No-Hitters

1904	Cy Young (perfect game)
	Jesse Tannehill
1905	Bill Dinneen
1908	Cy Young
1911	Joe Wood
1916	George Foster
	Dutch Leonard
1917	Ernie Shore (perfect game)
1918	Dutch Leonard
1919	Ray Caldwell
1923	Howard Ehmke
1956	Mel Parnell
1962	Earl Wilson
	Bill Monbouquette
1965	Dave Morehead

20-Game Winners

1902	Bill Dinneen	21–21
1903	Cy Young	28–9
	Bill Dinneen	21–13
	Long John Hughes	20–7
1904	Cy Young	26–16
	Bill Dinneen	23–14
	Jesse Tannehill	21–11
1905	Jesse Tannehill	22–9
1907	Cy Young	22–15
1908	Cy Young	21–11
1911	Joe Wood	23–17
1912	Joe Wood	34–5
	Buck O'Brien	20–13
	Hugh Bedient	20–9
1914	Ray Collins	20–13
1916	Babe Ruth	23–12
1917	Babe Ruth	24–13
	Carl Mays	22–9
1918	Carl Mays	21–13
1921	Sad Sam Jones	23–16
1923	Howard Ehmke	20–17

1935	Wes Ferrell	25–14
	Lefty Grove	20–12
1936	Wes Ferrell	20–15
1942	Tex Hughson	22–6
1945	Boo Ferriss	21–10
1946	Boo Ferriss	25–6
	Tex Hughson	20–11
1949	Mel Parnell	25–7
	Ellis Kinder	23–6
1953	Mel Parnell	21–8
1963	Bill Monbouquette	20–10
1967	Jim Lonborg	22–9
1973	Luis Tiant	20–13
1974	Luis Tiant	22–13
1976	Luis Tiant	21–12
1978	Dennis Eckersley	20–8
1986	Roger Clemens	24–4
1987	Roger Clemens	20–9

30-Game Winners

1901	Cy Young	33–10
1902	Cy Young	32–11
1912	Joe Wood	34–5

RECORD HOLDERS LIST

1	Cy Young	31
2	Ellis Kinder	15
3	Dick Radatz	13
4	Charley Hall	12
5	Joe Wood	8
6	Carl Mays	5
6	Wilcy Moore	5

6	Ted Lewis	5
9	Tony Welzer	4
9	Emerson Dickman	4
9	Bill Dinneen	4
12	Frank Arellanes	3
12	Dutch Leonard	3
12	Mike Fornieles	3
12	Joe Harris	3
12	George Winter	3
12	Tex Pruiett	3
12	Mace Brown	3
12	Joe Heving	3
12	Ike Delock	3
12	Bob Stanley	3
22	Howard Ehmke	2
22	Ralph Glaze	2
22	Hugh Bedient	2
22	Bill Campbell	2
22	Jack Lamabe	2
22	Johnny Welch	2
28	Red Ruffing	1
28	Babe Ruth	1
28	Wes Ferrell	1
28	Jack Wilson	1
28	Mel Parnell	1
28	Earl Wilson	1
28	Slim Harriss	1
28	Jesse Tannehill	1
28	Ed Cicotte	1
28	Benn Karr	1
28	Jim Willoughby	1
28	Calvin Schiraldi	1
28	Mike Ryba	1
28	Roger Clemens	1

SUMMARY AND HIGHLIGHTS

It should come as no surprise that Cy Young is at the top of the records list. Young has long been considered one of the greatest pitchers in baseball history.

Cy Young was a mountain of a man in his day. Standing 6′ 2″ and weighing 210 pounds, he was much bigger than the average player of his time.

His career began in 1890 with Cleveland of the National League, where he enjoyed eight outstanding seasons and averaged 28 wins. He was then traded to St. Louis, where he continued his success by winning 26 and 20 games before being sought out by Ban Johnson's raiders of the newly formed American League in 1901. Young was one of 111 players taken from the National League. Ban Johnson had attempted to honor the National Agreement, under which all organized baseball operated, but declared war on the National League after they had invited him to a league meeting, left him standing alone in a hallway, and then abandoned him there after the meeting was over.

It was easy for Johnson to raid the National League because the owners had refused to raise the salary ceiling of $2,400.

Cy Young was bought from the St. Louis Cardinals for $3,500 and paid $4,000, and accepted the challenge of the American League by winning a record 33 games in 1901 and then following with seasons of 32, 28, 26, 18, 13, 22, and 21 wins before being traded to Cleveland in 1909. In return for the aging pitcher Boston received Charlie Chech, Jack Ryan, and $12,500. Neither team really benefited from the trade, as Young went 29–29 during

---

RECORD PROFILES
CY YOUNG
SEASON PITCHING RECORDS

1901	Most Appearances	43	1 year before broken
	Most Starts	41	1 year before broken
	Most Complete Games	38	1 year before broken
	Most Wins	33	11 years before broken
	Highest Winning Percentage	.767	11 years before broken
	Lowest ERA	1.62	13 years before broken
	Most Innings	371	1 year before broken
	Most Hits Allowed	324	1 year before broken
	Most Strikeouts	158	1 year before broken
	Most Shutouts	5	2 years before broken
	Most Relief Wins	2	4 years before broken
	Most Wins Plus Saves	2	2 years before broken
1902	Most Appearances	45	18 years before broken
	Most Starts	43	**NEVER BROKEN**
	Most Complete Games	41	**NEVER BROKEN**
	Most Innings	386	**NEVER BROKEN**
	Most Hits Allowed	337	**NEVER BROKEN**
	Most Strikeouts	166	1 year before broken
1903	Most Strikeouts	183	1 year before broken
	Most Shutouts	7	1 year before broken
	Most Relief Wins	2	2 years before broken
	Most Wins Plus Saves	4	2 years before broken
	Most Saves	2	4 years before broken
1904	Most Strikeouts	203	1 year before broken
	Most Shutouts	10	**NEVER BROKEN**
	Most Relief Wins	2	1 year before broken
1905	Most Strikeouts	208	6 years before broken
	Most Relief Wins	5	5 years before broken
	Most Wins Plus Saves	5	4 years before broken
1906	Most Saves	2	1 year before broken
1907	Most Saves	3	2 years before broken

the last two and a half years of his career while Chech and Ryan played only one year with Boston and had a combined 11–8 mark.

Before leaving Boston, Cy Young placed his name in the record book an amazing 31 times. This is almost twice as many records as any other Red Sox hurler. Even though Young's records are over 80 years old, five of them still remain unbroken. It is very unlikely that modern-day pitchers will ever be allowed to start 43 games, complete 41, or work 386 innings in one season, as did this tireless hurler. One of the more interesting facts about Cy Young is that of all the years and games (906) he took the mound, never once did he ever have a trainer rub his arm, either before or after a game!

Since Young's departure the Red Sox have never had a righthanded

CY YOUNG

DICK RADATZ

RECORD PROFILE
DICK RADATZ
SEASON RELIEF PITCHING RECORDS

Year	Record	Value	Status
1962	Most Strikeouts	144	1 year before broken
1963	Most Wins	15	1 year before broken
	Most Strikeouts	162	1 year before broken
	Most Wins Plus Saves	40	1 year before broken
1964	Most Appearances	79	**NEVER BROKEN**
	Most Relief Games	79	**NEVER BROKEN**
	Most Wins	16	**NEVER BROKEN**
	Most Losses	9	1 year before broken
	Most Saves	29	13 years before broken
	Most Innings	157	18 years before broken
	Most Bases on Balls	58	13 years before broken
	Most Strikeouts	181	**NEVER BROKEN**
1965	Most Losses	11	11 years before broken

pitcher like him. Boo Ferriss showed great potential in 1945 and 1946, when he won 46 games in his first two seasons. But arm problems hit him, and his short career ended with a brilliant 65–30 mark. The club traded away outstanding pitchers in Carl Mays, Waite Hoyt, Sam Jones, Joe Bush, and Red Ruffing, and while three of them made it into the Hall of Fame, none were of the caliber of Cy Young. But in 1984 a 6' 3", 193-pound right-hander by the name of Roger Clemens put on a Red Sox uniform and, after getting off to a slow start, excited Boston fans by becoming their first 20-game winner in 8 years. Roger won 24 and lost 4 in 1986 and was 20–9 in 1987. In doing so, he won the Cy Young award 2 years in a row. Clemens was the second American League pitcher to win back-to-back honors—Jim Palmer of Baltimore was the only previous AL pitcher to do it, in 1975 and 1976. (Sandy Koufax of the National League also did it, in 1965 and 1966.)

In Clemens's sensational 1986 season, he struck out 20 batters in one nine-inning game to set a new record. Steve Carlton had 19 strikeouts in 1969, Nolan Ryan did it in 1974, Tom Seaver did it in 1970, and two old-timers, Hugh Daily and Charles Sweeney, did it way back in 1884.

Another marvelous starting pitcher to star for Boston was "Smokey" Joe Wood. When asked if he could throw harder than Joe Wood, Walter Johnson replied, "No one can throw faster than Joe Wood."

Smokey Joe won 23 games in 1911 and had his best season in 1912, when he set an all-time Boston record by winning 34 and losing only five games. Wood completed 35 of the 38 games he started and won 34 while only losing five for a record-breaking winning percentage of .872. No Red Sox pitcher has won 34 games since, and it is unlikely that this marvelous achievement will ever be topped. In this sensational season Wood tied Cy Young in shutouts with ten, and only Roger Clemens with 8 in 1988 came close to breaking their shutout records.

Because of Cy Young's tremendous success, starting pitchers who followed had extremely difficult times in getting into the record book. Dutch Leonard was one of the few who improved upon one of Young's marks when in 1914 he posted a Major League ERA record of 1.01. Leonard won 19 and lost five while spinning seven shutouts.

Young set five consecutive strikeout records from 1901 through 1905 and became the first Boston hurler to whiff 200 batters in a season. In 1904 Cy put down 203 batters, and he sent 208 of them back to their dugouts in 1905. Joe Wood improved the record to 231 in 1911 and to 258 in 1912. Roger Clemens came very close to breaking Wood's mark in 1987, when he fanned 256 batters. He became the new strikeout king in 1988 with 291.

Ellis Kinder and Dick Radatz stand out as two of the greatest Red Sox relief pitchers. Kinder is second to Young's 31 records with 15, while Radatz was responsible for 13 fabulous records.

Relief pitching records begin with those who appeared in a minimum of 25 games, and Charley Hall was the first to work in 25 or more games, in 1913.

PITCHERS SEASON BATTING RECORDS

Most At Bats

1901	Cy Young	153
1918	Babe Ruth	†317
1919	**Babe Ruth**	**†432**

Most Hits

1901	Cy Young	32
1902	Cy Young	34
1903	Cy Young	44
1918	Babe Ruth	†95
1919	**Babe Ruth**	**†139**

† *Note:* In 1918, Babe Ruth pitched in 20 games and appeared as a non-pitcher in 72 others. In 1919, he pitched in 17 games and appeared as a non-pitcher in 128 others. These statistics represent his complete year's achievements.

Most Home Runs

1901	George Winter	1
1902	Cy Young	1
1903	Cy Young	1
	Tom Hughes	1
1904	Cy Young	1
1905	Cy Young	2
1910	Ed Karger	2
1911	Joe Wood	2
1918	Babe Ruth	*†11
1919	**Babe Ruth**	***†29**

Highest Batting Average (Minimum 100 At Bats)

1901	Cy Young	.209
1902	Cy Young	.230
1903	Cy Young	.321
1917	Babe Ruth	.325
1921	Joe Bush	.325
1935	**Wes Ferrell**	**.347**

SUMMARY AND HIGHLIGHTS

Cy Young was not only the first great Boston pitcher, he was also the best hitting pitcher until Babe Ruth came along. "The Cyclone," as he was called, was the first Red Sox pitcher to hit two home runs in one season and bat over .300. The above-.300 batting average came in 1903, when baseball's winningest pitcher hit safely 44 times as he batted a smart .321. The year was 1905 when he made history as the club's greatest home run hitting pitcher.

Young later had to share this honor with Ed Karger and Joe Wood, who both would also hit two round-trippers in one season.

But it was the great Babe Ruth who set the records that will most likely never be broken. In 1918 the slugging pitcher boomed 11 big ones out of the park and became baseball's first and only pitcher to lead the league in home runs. It was a year in which the Babe won 13 while dropping seven in the 20 games he pitched. Perhaps it is not fair to consider him a pitcher, because he also played 59 games in the outfield and 13 at first base. But let's leave that decision up to the rules committee.

Ruth continued to pitch and play the field in 1919, and in addition to his 17 games on the mound the famous new slugger put in 111 games in the outfield and four at first base.

After only ten at bats in 1914, Ruth batted over .300 for the first time in 1915. He slipped to .272 the following year, before starting a string of 8 years in which he would bat over .300. After a .290 season in 1925 (when he was ill), the Babe put together another eight years of batting over .300.

But the Babe wasn't the only Red Sox pitcher who could hit. Joe Bush tied his batting average record with .325 in 1921, and Wes Ferrell has the club record with a scorching .347 in 1935. Ferrell was an outstanding hitting pitcher who had 52 hits (with seven home runs) in 150 at bats in the 1935 season.

DID YOU KNOW that the left field wall is closer than the 315 feet posted (309 feet)?

DID YOU KNOW that Fenway Park was named by owner John I. Taylor because it was in the Fenway section of Boston?

DID YOU KNOW that the first official game played at Fenway Park was on April 20, 1912, but was pushed off the front pages because of the sinking of the Titanic?

DID YOU KNOW that when Fenway Park was resodded in 1967, the old sod in left field was shipped to Carl Yastrzemski's home, where he still patrols it?

DID YOU KNOW that the first pinch hit registered in the American League was by Boston's Larry McLean on April 26, 1901? It was a double.

DID YOU KNOW that Boston's Pat Dougherty was the first player to hit two home runs in a World Series game (1903)?

DID YOU KNOW that when Cy Young pitched his perfect game in 1904, it only took 83 minutes?

DID YOU KNOW that the club was named the Red Sox in 1907, the year the Boston Braves stopped wearing red socks?

DID YOU KNOW that Cy Young pitched his last no-hitter when he was 41 years old and got three hits himself that day?

DID YOU KNOW that in Babe Ruth's first start as a pitcher, he was pitch hit for in the seventh inning?

CHAPTER III

SEASON FIELDING RECORDS

FIELDING QUIZ

1. His nickname was Dr. Strangeglove, but this first baseman registered the second-most assists in Boston history. Who was he?
2. This fine Red Sox second baseman once made an unassisted triple play, and his 459 putouts have never been equalled. Name him.
3. Two Red Sox players have set the mark for highest fielding percentage at both shortstop and third base. Do you know them?
4. The Red Sox catcher with the highest fielding percentage broke a 49-year-old record. Can you name him?
5. Duffy Lewis set every positive record for fielding—at which position?

DID YOU KNOW that Carl Yastrzemski and Ken Harrelson are the only two Red Sox outfielders who have played full seasons without making an error?

DID YOU KNOW that Babe Ruth held the Red Sox fielding average record in left field for 38 years before it was broken by Ted Williams?

DID YOU KNOW that Tris Speaker established 9 batting and 5 fielding records in one season in center field?

FIRST BASE

Most Putouts

1901	Buck Freeman	1,278
1902	Candy LaChance	**1,544
1904	Candy LaChance	**1,691
1926	**Phil Todt**	**1,755**

Most Assists

1901	Buck Freeman	55
1903	Candy LaChance	57
1904	Candy LaChance	59
1906	Moose Grimshaw	64
1907	Bob Unglaub	84
1920	Stuffy McInnis	91
1921	Stuffy McInnis	102
1926	Phil Todt	126
1963	Dick Stuart	134
1985	**Bill Buckner**	**184**

Most Errors

1901	Buck Freeman	*36

Fewest Errors

1901	Buck Freeman	36
1902	Candy LaChance	27
1903	Candy LaChance	25
1904	Candy LaChance	14
1917	Dick Hoblitzell	14
1918	Stuffy McInnis	9
1919	Stuffy McInnis	7
1920	Stuffy McInnis	7
1921	**Stuffy McInnis**	**1**

Most Double Plays

1901	Buck Freeman	71
1902	Candy LaChance	80
1919	Stuffy McInnis	84
1920	Stuffy McInnis	101
1921	Stuffy McInnis	109
1925	Phil Todt	126
1929	Phil Todt	128
1938	Jimmy Foxx	153
1946	**Rudy York**	**154**

Most Chances Per Game

1901	Buck Freeman	10.7
1902	Candy LaChance	*11.7
1918	Stuffy McInnis	12.2
1926	**Phil Todt**	**12.4**

Most Total Chances

1901	Buck Freeman	1,369
1902	Candy LaChance	*1,617
1904	Candy LaChance	*1,764
1926	**Phil Todt**	**1,903**

Highest Fielding Percentage

1901	Buck Freeman	.974
1902	Candy LaChance	.983
1903	Candy LaChance	.984
1904	Candy LaChance	*.992
1918	Stuffy McInnis	.992
1919	Stuffy McInnis	.995
1920	Stuffy McInnis	.996
1921	**Stuffy McInnis**	****.999**

SECOND BASE

Most Putouts

1901	Hobe Ferris	359
1904	Hobe Ferris	366
1907	Hobe Ferris	*424
1924	**Bill Wambsganss**	**459**

Most Assists

1901	Hobe Ferris	450
1902	Hobe Ferris	*461
1922	Del Pratt	484
1924	**Bill Wambsganss**	**490**
1943	**Bobby Doerr**	**490**

Most Errors

1901	**Hobe Ferris**	**61**

---

* American League Record
** Major League Record
*** Unbroken Major League Record

Sam Snead's response to Ted Williams, who had said that hitting a baseball was tougher than hitting a golf ball: "Yeah but you don't have to play your foul balls like we have to."

Fewest Errors

1901	Hobe Ferris	61
1902	Hobe Ferris	39
1903	Hobe Ferris	39
1904	Hobe Ferris	33
1905	Hobe Ferris	30
1906	Hobe Ferris	29
1913	Steve Yerkes	25
1917	Jack Barry	14
1936	Oscar Melillo	10
1943	Bobby Doerr	9
1948	**Bobby Doerr**	**6**
1973	**Doug Griffin**	**6**

Most Double Plays

1901	Hobe Ferris	*68
1921	Del Pratt	90
1924	Bill Wambsganss	98
1938	Bobby Doerr	118
1940	Bobby Doerr	118
1943	Bobby Doerr	132
1949	Bobby Doerr	134

Most Chances Per Game

1901	Hobe Ferris	*6.3
1924	**Bill Wambsganss**	**6.4**
1926	**Bill Regan**	**6.4**
1935	**Oscar Melillo**	**6.4**

Most Total Chances

1901	Hobe Ferris	*870
1907	Hobe Ferris	*913
1924	**Bill Wambsganss**	**986**

Highest Fielding Percentage

1901	Hobe Ferris	.930
1902	Hobe Ferris	.952
1904	Hobe Ferris	.962
1907	Hobe Ferris	.967
1917	Jack Barry	.974
1936	Oscar Melillo	.980
1943	Bobby Doerr	.990
1948	**Bobby Doerr**	****.993**

Tommy Henrich: "Bobby Doerr was one of the few guys who played the game hard and came away with no enemies."

SHORTSTOP

Most Putouts

1901	Freddy Parent	260
1902	Freddy Parent	287
1903	Freddy Parent	296
1904	Freddy Parent	327
1908	Heinie Wagner	373
1921	**Everett Scott**	**380**

Most Assists

1901	Freddy Parent	446
1902	Freddy Parent	*496
1908	**Heinie Wagner**	**569**

Most Errors

1901	Freddy Parent	63
1904	Freddy Parent	63
1905	**Freddy Parent**	**66**

Fewest Errors

1901	Freddy Parent	63
1902	Freddy Parent	58
1903	Freddy Parent	57
1906	Freddy Parent	56
1907	Heinie Wagner	50
1909	Heinie Wagner	50
1911	Steve Yerkes	47
1913	Heinie Wagner	39
1914	Everett Scott	39
1916	Everett Scott	19
1918	Everett Scott	17
1919	Everett Scott	17
1947	Johnny Pesky	16
1950	Vern Stephens	13
1968	**Rico Petrocelli**	**12**

Most Double Plays

1901	Freddy Parent	52
1902	Freddy Parent	60
1917	Everett Scott	64
1920	Everett Scott	64
1921	Everett Scott	94
1938	Joe Cronin	110
1945	Eddie Lake	112
1948	Vern Stephens	113
1949	Vern Stephens	128
1980	**Rick Burleson**	*****147**

Most Chances Per Game

1901	Freddy Parent	5.6
1902	Freddy Parent	6.1
1907	**Heinie Wagner**	****6.6**
1908	**Heinie Wagner**	****6.6**

Most Total Chances

1901	Freddy Parent	769
1902	Freddy Parent	841
1904	Freddy Parent	883
1908	**Heinie Wagner**	****1,003**

Highest Fielding Percentage

1901	Freddy Parent	.918
1902	Freddy Parent	.931
1906	Freddy Parent	.933
1908	Heinie Wagner	.939
1914	Everett Scott	.949
1916	Everett Scott	.967
1918	Everett Scott	**.976
1919	Everett Scott	**.976
1947	Johnny Pesky	.976
1950	**Vern Stephens**	**.981**
1969	**Rico Petrocelli**	**.981**
1978	**Rick Burleson**	**.981**

THIRD BASE

Most Putouts

1901	Jimmy Collins	203

Most Assists

1901	Jimmy Collins	*328
1939	Jim Tabor	338
1957	Frank Malzone	370
1958	**Frank Malzone**	**378**

Most Errors

1901	Jimmy Collins	50

Fewest Errors

1901	Jimmy Collins	50
1902	Jimmy Collins	19
1919	Ossie Vitt	13
1950	Johnny Pesky	11
1953	George Kell	10
1955	**Grady Hatton**	**8**

Most Double Plays

1901	Jimmy Collins	24
1916	Larry Gardner	24
1919	Ossie Vitt	24
1926	Fred Haney	30
1928	Buddy Myer	35
1948	Johnny Pesky	35
1949	Johnny Pesky	48
1977	**Butch Hobson**	*****57**

Most Chances Per Game

1901	Jimmy Collins	*4.2

Most Total Chances

1901	Jimmy Collins	*581

Highest Fielding Percentage

1901	Jimmy Collins	.914
1902	Jimmy Collins	*.954
1919	Ossie Vitt	.967
1928	Buddy Myer	.969
1949	Johnny Pesky	.970
1950	Johnny Pesky	.974
1955	**Grady Hatton**	**.976**
1971	**Rico Petrocelli**	**.976**

CATCHING

Most Putouts

1901	Lou Criger	300
1902	Lou Criger	330
1903	Lou Criger	491
1904	Lou Criger	502
1905	Lou Criger	539
1936	Rick Ferrell	556
1953	Sammy White	588
1954	Sammy White	677
1964	**Bob Tillman**	**897**

Most Assists

1901	Lou Criger	109
1902	Lou Criger	117
1903	**Lou Criger**	***156**

DID YOU KNOW that Jackie Robinson had a tryout with the Red Sox before being signed by the Dodgers (1945)?

Most Errors
| 1901 | Ossee Schreckengost | *30 |

Fewest Errors
1901	Lou Criger	14
1903	Lou Criger	14
1904	Lou Criger	12
1911	Bill Carrigan	12
1913	Bill Carrigan	11
1914	Bill Carrigan	7
1926	Alex Gaston	7
1931	Charlie Berry	6
1933	Rick Ferrell	6
1934	Rick Ferrell	6
1937	**Gene DeSautels**	**4**
1941	**Frankie Pytlak**	**4**

Most Double Plays
1901	Lou Criger	11
1907	Lou Criger	12
1910	Bill Carrigan	12
1915	Hick Cady	12
1919	Wally Schang	15
1920	Roxy Walters	15
1922	**Muddy Ruel**	**17**

Most Chances Per Game
1901	Lou Criger	6.2
1903	Lou Criger	*6.9
1911	Bill Carrigan	7.0
1964	**Bob Tillman**	**7.3**

Most Total Chances
1901	Lou Criger	423
1902	Lou Criger	463
1903	Lou Criger	*661
1905	Lou Criger	706
1954	Sammy White	773
1964	**Bob Tillman**	**957**

Highest Fielding Percentage
1901	Lou Criger	.967
1903	Lou Criger	.979
1904	Lou Criger	.981
1914	Bill Carrigan	.984
1931	Charlie Berry	.985
1933	Rick Ferrell	.990
1934	Rick Ferrell	.990
1937	Gene DeSautels	.993
1986	**Rich Gedman**	**.994**

LEFT FIELD

Most Putouts
1901	Tommy Dowd	*288
1912	Duffy Lewis	301
1916	Duffy Lewis	306
1917	Duffy Lewis	324
1946	Ted Williams	325
1947	**Ted Williams**	**347**

Most Assists
1901	Tommy Dowd	11
1903	Pat Dougherty	16
1909	Harry Niles	20
1910	Duffy Lewis	*28
1913	**Duffy Lewis**	***29**

Most Errors
1901	Tommy Dowd	*20
1902	Pat Dougherty	20
1905	**Jesse Burkett**	**22**

Fewest Errors
1901	Tommy Dowd	20
1902	Pat Dougherty	20
1903	Pat Dougherty	14
1908	Jack Thoney	12
1909	Harry Niles	11
1916	Duffy Lewis	10
1917	Duffy Lewis	10
1919	Babe Ruth	2
1957	Ted Williams	1
1977	**Carl Yastrzemski**	***0**

Most Double Plays
1901	Tommy Dowd	3
1903	Pat Dougherty	3
1907	Jimmy Barrett	5
1910	**Duffy Lewis**	***9**

Most Chances Per Game
1901	Tommy Dowd	*2.3
1908	Jack Thoney	2.3
1917	Duffy Lewis	2.4
1922	**Mike Menosky**	**2.5**

Most Total Chances
1901	Tommy Dowd	*319
1912	Duffy Lewis	342
1917	Duffy Lewis	354
1947	**Ted Williams**	**366**

Highest Fielding Percentage

1901	Tommy Dowd	.937
1903	Pat Dougherty	.952
1909	Harry Niles	.952
1913	Duffy Lewis	.960
1916	Duffy Lewis	.970
1917	Duffy Lewis	.972
1919	Babe Ruth	**.992
1957	Ted Williams	.995
1977	**Carl Yastrzemski**	***1.000

CENTER FIELD

Most Putouts

1902	Chick Stahl	277
1904	Chick Stahl	293
1906	Chick Stahl	*344
1912	Tris Speaker	372
1913	Tris Speaker	374
1914	Tris Speaker	**423
1925	Ira Flagstead	429
1930	Tommy Oliver	477
1948	**Dom DiMaggio**	*503

Most Assists

1901	Chick Stahl	12
1902	Chick Stahl	15
1906	Chick Stahl	24
1909	**Tris Speaker**	*35
1912	**Tris Speaker**	*35

Most Errors

1901	Chick Stahl	13
1906	Chick Stahl	15
1910	Tris Speaker	16
1912	Tris Speaker	18
1913	**Tris Speaker**	*25

Fewest Errors

1901	Chick Stahl	13
1902	Chick Stahl	12
1904	Chick Stahl	12
1905	Chick Stahl	6
1908	Denny Sullivan	4
1918	Amos Strunk	3
1931	Tommy Oliver	3
1955	Jimmy Piersall	3
1974	Rick Miller	3
1977	**Fred Lynn**	2
1980	**Fred Lynn**	2

Most Double Plays

1901	Chick Stahl	3
1905	Chick Stahl	4
1906	Chick Stahl	9
1909	**Tris Speaker**	*12
1914	**Tris Speaker**	*12

Most Chances Per Game

1901	Chick Stahl	2.3
1906	Chick Stahl	*2.5
1909	Tris Speaker	2.6
1910	Tris Speaker	2.7
1912	Tris Speaker	2.8
1913	Tris Speaker	*3.1
1925	Ira Flagstead	3.2
1930	Tommy Oliver	3.2
1944	Charly Metkovich	3.2
1947	Dom DiMaggio	3.3
1948	**Dom DiMaggio**	*3.4

Most Total Chances

1901	Chick Stahl	302
1904	Chick Stahl	311
1906	Chick Stahl	*383
1912	Tris Speaker	425
1913	Tris Speaker	*429
1914	Tris Speaker	**467
1930	Tommy Oliver	495
1948	**Dom DiMaggio**	*526

Highest Fielding Percentage

1901	Chick Stahl	.957
1904	Chick Stahl	.961
1905	Chick Stahl	.977
1908	Denny Sullivan	.981
1918	Amos Strunk	*.988
1931	Tommy Oliver	**.993
1955	Jimmy Piersall	.993
1977	Fred Lynn	.994
1980	Fred Lynn	.994

DID YOU KNOW that Tris Speaker was called the Gray Eagle because of his prematurely white hair?

DID YOU KNOW that Babe Ruth and Joe Wood are the only two players ever to play in a World Series as both pitcher and outfielder?

RIGHT FIELD

Most Putouts

1901	Charlie Hemphill	188
1902	Buck Freeman	222
1910	Harry Hooper	241
1913	Harry Hooper	248
1915	Harry Hooper	255
1916	Harry Hooper	266
1920	Mike Menosky	281
1939	Ted Williams	318
1953	Jimmy Piersall	352
1971	**Reggie Smith**	**386**

Most Assists

1901	Charlie Hemphill	22
1910	Harry Hooper	30
1923	**Ira Flagstead**	**33**

Most Errors

1901	Charlie Hemphill	17
1910	Harry Hooper	18
1933	**Roy Johnson**	**25**

Fewest Errors

1901	Charlie Hemphill	17
1902	Buck Freeman	14
1904	Buck Freeman	11
1907	Bunk Congalton	6
1919	Harry Hooper	6
1924	Ike Boone	5
1937	Ben Chapman	4
1944	Pete Fox	3
1947	Sam Mele	2
1964	Lee Thomas	1
1968	**Ken Harrelson**	***0

Most Double Plays

1901	Charlie Hemphill	4
1904	Buck Freeman	4
1907	Bunk Congalton	4
1908	Doc Gessler	4
1910	Harry Hooper	7
1913	Harry Hooper	7
1915	Harry Hooper	7
1918	**Harry Hooper**	**8**
1921	Shano Collins	8
1923	Ira Flagstead	8
1928	Doug Taitt	8
1975	Dwight Evans	8

Most Chances Per Game

1901	Charlie Hemphill	1.7
1902	Buck Freeman	1.8
1905	Kip Selbach	1.8
1910	Harry Hooper	1.9
1913	Harry Hooper	1.9
1914	Harry Hooper	1.9
1915	Harry Hooper	1.9
1916	Harry Hooper	2.0
1918	Harry Hooper	2.0
1920	Mike Menosky	2.2
1922	Shano Collins	2.3
1923	Ira Flagstead	2.6
1933	Roy Johnson	2.6
1940	**Dom DiMaggio**	**2.8**
1973	**Reggie Smith**	**2.8**

Most Total Chances

1901	Charlie Hemphill	227
1902	Buck Freeman	251
1910	Harry Hooper	289
1916	Harry Hooper	295
1920	Mike Menosky	310
1933	Roy Johnson	319
1939	Ted Williams	348
1953	Jimmy Piersall	372
1971	**Reggie Smith**	**415**

Highest Fielding Percentage

1901	Charlie Hemphill	.925
1902	Buck Freeman	.944
1904	Buck Freeman	.954
1907	Bunk Congalton	.969
1914	Harry Hooper	.973
1919	Harry Hooper	.979
1937	Ben Chapman	.985
1944	Pete Fox	.987
1947	Sam Mele	.992
1964	Lee Thomas	.995
1968	**Ken Harrelson**	***1.000

RECORD HOLDERS LIST

1	Chick Stahl	23
1	Freddy Parent	23
3	Lou Criger	22
4	Harry Hooper	21
5	Hobe Ferris	20
6	Tris Speaker	17
7	Buck Freeman	16

8	Candy LaChance	14		38	Sam Mele	2
8	Stuffy McInnis	14		38	Jack Barry	2
8	Duffy Lewis	14		38	Lee Thomas	2
11	Everett Scott	12		38	Denny Sullivan	2
12	Jimmy Collins	10		38	Amos Strunk	2
13	Bobby Doerr	9		38	Ben Chapman	2
14	Charlie Hemphill	8		38	Ken Harrelson	2
14	Tommy Dowd	8		38	Del Pratt	2
14	Heinie Wagner	8		38	Frank Malzone	2
17	Ted Williams	7		38	Shano Collins	2
17	Johnny Pesky	7		58	Roxy Walters	1
19	Pat Dougherty	6		58	Rick Miller	1
19	Bill Carrigan	6		58	Eddie Lake	1
19	Phil Todt	6		58	Jim Tabor	1
22	Dom DiMaggio	5		58	Fred Haney	1
22	Ira Flagstead	5		58	Kip Selbach	1
22	Rick Ferrell	5		58	Hick Cady	1
22	Tommy Oliver	5		58	Muddy Ruel	1
22	Bill Wambsganss	5		58	Charley Metkovich	1
27	Jimmy Piersall	4		58	Moose Grimshaw	1
27	Fred Lynn	4		58	Bob Unglaub	1
27	Harry Niles	4		58	Dick Stuart	1
27	Vern Stephens	4		58	Joe Cronin	1
27	Mike Menosky	4		58	Steve Yerkes	1
32	Roy Johnson	3		58	Bill Regan	1
32	Sammy White	3		58	Rudy York	1
32	Bob Tillman	3		58	Jimmy Foxx	1
32	Reggie Smith	3		58	Ike Boone	1
32	Oscar Melillo	3		58	Jack Thoney	1
32	Ossie Vitt	3		58	Jesse Burkett	1
38	Charlie Berry	2		58	Wally Schang	1
38	Rico Petrocelli	2		58	Alex Gaston	1
38	Grady Hatton	2		58	Larry Gardner	1
38	Rick Burleson	2		58	Frank Pytlak	1
38	Buddy Myer	2		58	Rich Gedman	1
38	Babe Ruth	2		58	Jimmy Barrett	1
38	Carl Yastrzemski	2		58	Bill Buckner	1
38	Bunk Congalton	2		58	Doug Taitt	1
38	Gene DeSautels	2		58	Doc Gessler	1
38	Pete Fox	2		58	Dwight Evans	1

SUMMARY AND HIGHLIGHTS

Do not be misled by the great number of records established by the players who were on the original team in 1901. It was inevitable for them to accumulate records in abundance, since no marks stood before them. Subsequently all they had to do to create records was to improve upon their own achievements.

STUFFY McINNIS

RECORD PROFILE
STUFFY McINNIS
SEASON FIELDING RECORDS
FIRST BASE

1918	Most Chances Per Game	12.2	8 years before broken
	Highest Fielding Percentage	.992	1 year before broken
	Fewest Errors	9	1 year before broken
1919	Highest Fielding Percentage	.995	1 year before broken
	Fewest Errors	7	1 year before broken
	Most Double Plays	84	1 year before broken
1920	Highest Fielding Percentage	.996	1 year before broken
	Fewest Errors	7	1 year before broken
	Most Double Plays	101	1 year before broken
	Most Assists	91	1 year before broken
1921	Highest Fielding Percentage	.999	**NEVER BROKEN**
	Fewest Errors	1	**NEVER BROKEN**
	Most Double Plays	109	4 years before broken
	Most Assists	102	5 years before broken

It is interesting to see the improvements made by each player. At first base Candy LaChance went from 25 errors in 1903 to 14 in 1904. Stuffy McInnis must go down in history as the greatest-fielding Red Sox first baseman, as he made only one error in 1921.

When one considers the poor gloves used in his era, it is easy to see that McInnis's performance in 1921 was a great fielding feat. Even with the modern gloves that would follow, no Red Sox first basemen have matched this record. It is also important to note that McInnis's accomplishment was not just a lucky, one-time occurrence. Prior to his historic record, Stuffy tied LaChance's .992 fielding percentage mark, improved his own record to .995 in 1919, and then broke it again in 1920 with a .996 before being almost perfect in 1921 with his brilliant .999 average.

The improvement at second base was almost as dramatic. Hobe Ferris started things off with 61 big errors in 1901, and he improved himself by only making 29 errors in 1906. Since then Bobby Doerr and Doug Griffin have reduced the mark to six. Doerr, who recently was inducted into the Hall of Fame, had his best season in 1948, and his feat was so fine that it took Griffin and an even more modern glove 25 years just to tie his mark.

Shortstop is the most difficult position to play, as can be seen by the 63 errors put into the book by Freddy Parent in 1901. The dramatic improvement at this position took place in 1916, when Everett Scott dropped the errors mark from 39 down to 19. The record sits at 12 today.

After committing 50 errors at third base, player-manager Jimmy Collins recovered in 1902 by misplaying only 19 chances.

It is natural for outfielders to commit fewer errors than infielders. But not many players can boast of going through a full season without making a single error. Ken Harrelson was the first and only rightfielder to do it, in 1968, and Carl Yastrzemski completely tamed the "Green Monster" in 1977. Yaz was switched to first base and designated hitter, though, from that point until the end of his career in 1983.

An interesting drama unfolded in 1919, when Babe Ruth became an everyday player. After giving up pitching, the Babe took the left field position and ended up setting a new fielding percentage record of .992. This was not only a team record but a Major League record as well. It was the Babe's first experience at playing the outfield, and such a great athlete was he that he reduced the errors record from ten down to two.

Ruth's achievement was so great that it took 38 years before it would finally be broken. And it was broken by none other than Ted Williams. Many had called Williams a poor fielder. But the Thumper showed them by making only one error in 1957. It would take 21 years before Carl Yastrzemski would play a full season in left field without making an error.

Chick Stahl was a fine-fielding center fielder, and he committed only 13 errors in the first year of Boston's franchise. He then broke his own mark in 1905 with only six misplays. Amos Strunk was super in 1918 with only three errors, a feat that would take 59 years and a much better glove to

HARRY HOOPER

RECORD PROFILE
HARRY HOOPER
SEASON FIELDING RECORDS
RIGHT FIELD

1910	Most Chances Per Game	1.9	6 years before broken
	Most Total Chances	289	6 years before broken
	Most Errors	18	23 years before broken
	Most Double Plays	7	8 years before broken
	Most Putouts	241	3 years before broken
	Most Assists	30	13 years before broken
1913	Most Chances Per Game	1.9	3 years before broken
	Most Double Plays	7	5 years before broken
	Most Putouts	248	2 years before broken
1914	Most Chances Per Game	1.9	2 years before broken
	Highest Fielding Percentage	.973	5 years before broken
1915	Most Double Plays	7	3 years before broken
	Most Chances Per Game	1.9	1 year before broken
	Most Putouts	255	1 year before broken
1916	Most Chances Per Game	2.0	4 years before broken
	Most Putouts	266	4 years before broken
	Most Total Chances	295	4 years before broken
1918	Most Chances Per Game	2.0	2 years before broken
	Most Double Plays	8	**NEVER BROKEN**
1919	Highest Fielding Percentage	.979	18 years before broken
	Fewest Errors	6	5 years before broken

break. Fred Lynn had such a glove and a pair of good hands to go with it, and in 1977 he set the Red Sox fielding percentage record by making only two errors. To prove it was no fluke, Lynn duplicated his feat in 1980.

Charlie Hemphill was the original right fielder, and he did well in making only 17 errors. Buck Freeman, moving from first base, got the mark down to 11 by 1904, and Bunk Congalton cut it to six in 1907. Ken Harrelson was perfect in 1968, to become the first Red Sox outfielder to not make an error in a full season of play.

CHAPTER IV

ROOKIE BATTING RECORDS

BATTING QUIZ

1. Can you name the Red Sox rookie who played in all 162 games?
2. Two fine Red Sox rookies share the record for most at bats, with 646. Who are they?
3. Only one Red Sox rookie has ever belted more than 200 hits. Do you remember this pesky little hitter?
4. Ted Williams set a new Red Sox rookie doubles record in 1939, when he slammed 44 two-baggers. Who broke his record?
5. Ted Williams also set a new home run record in 1939, when he poled 31. Who is the present rookie home run champion?

DID YOU KNOW that Ted Williams established nine rookie records and that five of them still stand?

DID YOU KNOW that Freddy Parent was the first outstanding rookie? In the first year of the club's franchise, he created 13 marks.

DID YOU KNOW that little-known Russ Scarritt banged 17 triples in 1929 and that the record has never been broken?

Most Games

1901	Freddy Parent	138
	Hobe Ferris	138
1907	Denny Sullivan	144
1908	Harry Lord	145
1910	Duffy Lewis	151
1929	Russ Scarritt	151
1930	Tommy Oliver	154
1961	Chuck Schilling	158
1966	**George Scott**	***162

Most At Bats

1901	Hobe Ferris	523
1907	Denny Sullivan	551
1908	Harry Lord	558
1930	**Tommy Oliver**	646
1961	**Chuck Schilling**	646

Most Hits

1901	Freddy Parent	158
1924	Ike Boone	162
1930	Tommy Oliver	189
1942	**Johnny Pesky**	205

Most Singles

1901	Freddy Parent	122
1902	Pat Dougherty	132
1930	Tommy Oliver	153
1942	**Johnny Pesky**	*165

Most Doubles

1901	Freddy Parent	23
1910	Duffy Lewis	29
1924	Ike Boone	29
1930	Tommy Oliver	34
1939	Ted Williams	44
1975	**Fred Lynn**	*47

Most Triples

| 1901 | Hobe Ferris | *15 |
| **1929** | **Russ Scarritt** | 17 |

Most Home Runs

1901	Freddy Parent	4
1905	Moose Grimshaw	4
1910	Duffy Lewis	*8
1924	Ike Boone	13
1939	Ted Williams	31
1950	**Walt Dropo**	34

Highest Home Run Percentage

1901	Freddy Parent	0.8
1902	Harry Gleason	0.8
1905	Moose Grimshaw	1.4
1910	Duffy Lewis	1.5
1915	Babe Ruth	*4.3
1939	Ted Williams	5.5
1950	Walt Dropo	6.1
1987	**Sam Horn**	8.9

Most Extra Base Hits

1901	Freddy Parent	36
1910	Duffy Lewis	44
1924	Ike Boone	45
1939	**Ted Williams**	86

Most Total Bases

1901	Freddy Parent	211
1910	Duffy Lewis	220
1924	Ike Boone	236
1939	**Ted Williams**	344

Most Runs

| 1901 | Freddy Parent | 87 |
| **1939** | **Ted Williams** | 131 |

Most RBIs

1901	Hobe Ferris	63
1910	Duffy Lewis	68
1924	Ike Boone	96
1939	**Ted Williams**	***145

* American League Record
** Major League Record
*** Unbroken Major League Record

Ty Cobb: "Ted Williams was the best natural hitter I ever saw, and I saw them all."

Mickey Mantle: "Ted Williams was the best hitter I ever saw. He attacked the pitch and exploded at the ball."

Most Strikeouts

1901–12	Statistics Not Kept	
1913	Hal Janvrin	27
1914	Everett Scott	43
1927	Jack Rothrock	46
1931	Urbane Pickering	53
1935	Babe Dahlgren	67
1950	Walt Dropo	75
1952	Dick Gernert	83
1955	Norm Zauchin	105
1966	**George Scott**	****152**

Most Bases on Balls

1901	Freddy Parent	41
1902	Pat Dougherty	42
1907	Denny Sullivan	44
1911	Steve Yerkes	52
1924	Ike Boone	55
1932	Marv Olson	61
1939	**Ted Williams**	***107**

Most Stolen Bases

1901	Freddy Parent	16
1902	Pat Dougherty	20
1907	Heinie Wagner	20
1908	**Amby McConnell**	**32**

Highest Batting Average

1901	Freddy Parent	.306
1902	Pat Dougherty	*.342
1982	**Wade Boggs**	**.349**

Highest Slugging Percentage

1901	Freddy Parent	.408
1915	Babe Ruth	.576
1939	Ted Williams	.609
1987	**Sam Horn**	**.698**

Most Pinch At Bats

1901	None	
1902	Harry Gleason	*8
1905	Bob Unglaub	12
1908	Gavvy Cravath	14
1916	Babe Ruth	19
1917	Chick Shorten	24
1924	Phil Todt	30
1925	**Tex Vache**	**49**

DID YOU KNOW that Ted Williams struck out his first two times up?

Most Pinch Hits

1901	None	
1902	Harry Gleason	**3
1905	Moose Grimshaw	3
1908	Amby McConnell	5
	Gavvy Cravath	5
1917	Chick Shorten	5
1923	Dick Reichle	5
1925	Tex Vache	10
1938	Red Nonnenkamp	10
1940	**Stan Spence**	**11**
1964	**Dalton Jones**	**11**

Highest Pinch Batting Average (Minimum 10 At Bats)

1902	Harry Gleason	**.300
1908	**Amby McConnell**	**.500**

RECORD HOLDERS LIST

1	Freddy Parent	13
2	Ted Williams	9
3	Duffy Lewis	7
3	Ike Boone	7
5	Tommy Oliver	5
6	Hobe Ferris	4
6	Pat Dougherty	4
8	Denny Sullivan	3
8	Moose Grimshaw	3
8	Walt Dropo	3
8	Harry Gleason	3
8	Babe Ruth	3
8	Amby McConnell	3
14	Sam Horn	2
14	Harry Lord	2
14	Chuck Schilling	2
14	George Scott	2
14	Johnny Pesky	2
14	Russ Scarritt	2
14	Gavvy Cravath	2
14	Tex Vache	2
14	Chick Shorten	2
23	Urbane Pickering	1
23	Fred Lynn	1
23	Hal Janvrin	1
23	Everett Scott	1
23	Jack Rothrock	1
23	Wade Boggs	1

23	Babe Dahlgren	1		23	Heinie Wagner	1
23	Dick Gernert	1		23	Bob Unglaub	1
23	Norm Zauchin	1		23	Red Nonnenkamp	1
23	Steve Yerkes	1		23	Stan Spence	1
23	Marv Olson	1		23	Dalton Jones	1

SUMMARY AND HIGHLIGHTS

Freddy Parent was Boston's first outstanding rookie, in 1901. He was Boston's first .300 hitter and set 13 of the original marks for future rookies to improve upon.

Ted Williams is in second place, with nine marvelous records. Ted is not only the greatest player in Red Sox history but also their greatest rookie. Of his nine records, five remain unbroken, as no other rookies have done better than the Thumper's 86 extra base hits, 344 total bases, 145 RBIs, 131 runs, and 107 bases on balls.

Prior to Ted Williams the most outstanding rookie was Tommy Oliver, who starred in 1930. "Ollie" slammed out 189 hits and put five new records in the book.

Fred Lynn had superstar written all over him when he arrived in 1975. He did not disappoint the Red Sox fans as he promptly stroked 175 hits and batted a satisfying .331, set a new doubles record with 47 (still unbroken), scored 103 runs, and slugged .566. The remarkable thing about Lynn's achievements was that they all led the league in their respective categories. That is quite a feat for a rookie. It is a rare occurrence when a rookie leads the league in slugging. What was even more rare was the fact that Lynn was voted the Rookie of the Year *and* MVP, which marked the first and only time in baseball history that a player had won both awards.

Lynn enjoyed 7 years with the Red Sox before being traded along with Steve Renko to the California Angels. In return the Red Sox received Frank Tanana, Jim Dorsey, and Joe Rudi. Lynn had been injury-prone, but he continues to play well. Tanana continues to pitch in the Major Leagues, while Dorsey and Rudi did not last long.

The home run record was originally set in 1901 by Freddy Parent. All it took was four round-trippers to win this first home run title. Three others improved the mark, but Ted Williams was the first solid rookie home run hitter. The Splendid Splinter smashed 31 balls over the right-field wall, a record that would last 11 years before big Walt Dropo put his 6' 5", 220-pound body to work by blasting 34 homers to become the new club leader. To this date no rookie has done better. The Red Sox fans thought they had a new superstar in their big man, but the sophomore jinx hit Dropo hard. He slumped to .239 with only 11 home runs in 1951, and after 37 games in 1952 "The Moose" was dealt to Detroit as part of the Johnny Pesky trade. From Detroit, Dropo went to Chicago and Cincinnati and ended his career with Baltimore. In all he played 13 seasons with 152 home runs and a batting average of .270.

TED WILLIAMS

RECORD PROFILE
TED WILLIAMS
ROOKIE BATTING RECORDS

1939			
	Most Doubles	44	36 years before broken
	Most Home Runs	31	11 years before broken
	Highest Home Run Percentage	5.5	11 years before broken
	Most Extra Base Hits	86	**NEVER BROKEN**
	Most Total Bases	344	**NEVER BROKEN**
	Most Runs	131	**NEVER BROKEN**
	Most RBIs	145	**NEVER BROKEN**
	Most Bases on Balls	107	**NEVER BROKEN**
	Highest Slugging Percentage	.609	48 years before broken

FREDDY PARENT

RECORD PROFILE
FREDDY PARENT
ROOKIE BATTING RECORDS

1901	Most Games	138	6 years before broken
	Most Hits	158	28 years before broken
	Most Singles	122	1 year before broken
	Most Doubles	23	9 years before broken
	Most Home Runs	4	9 years before broken
	Highest Home Run Percentage	0.8	1 year before broken
	Most Extra Base Hits	36	9 years before broken
	Most Total Bases	211	9 years before broken
	Most Runs	87	38 years before broken
	Most Bases on Balls	41	1 year before broken
	Most Stolen Bases	16	1 year before broken
	Highest Batting Average	.306	1 year before broken
	Highest Slugging Percentage	.408	15 years before broken

The longest unbroken rookie record belongs to a little-known player by the name of Amby McConnell, who stole 31 bases in 1908. Ellis Burks came the closest to breaking it, when he swiped 27 bases in 1987. In addition to his 31 stolen bases, McConnell had 140 hits and batted a respectable .279 but became another victim of the sophomore jinx in 1909. He batted just .238 and after only 12 games in 1910 was sent to Chicago. McConnell batted .280 for the White Sox but retired after that season.

When Ike Boone qualified for his rookie status in 1924, he added his name to the record book seven times. Although not records, Boone's smart .333 batting average and his .486 slugging percentage concluded a fine rookie season.

Boone almost did as well in his second year and was not affected by the sophomore jinx as he rapped 157 hits and batted .330 while slugging .479. But that was all the opportunity he would have with the Red Sox, who traded him to the White Sox the following year. Boone played only 29 games with his new team and was then traded to the Dodgers, where he played only 59 games in the next 3 years before retiring.

Freddy Parent batted .306 in 1901 to become the first .300 hitter. He was followed by Pat Dougherty, who was brilliant in 1902 with a solid .342 mark. Dougherty's record stood for 80 years before present-day superstar Wade Boggs served notice by hitting at a .349 clip in 1982.

Tex Vache has been the most active rookie pinch hitter. He strolled to the plate 49 times in 1925 and is still the leader. Vache also became the first to manage ten pinch hits. The present record is 11 pinch hits and is shared by Stan Spence and Dalton Jones.

CHAPTER V

ROOKIE PITCHING RECORDS

PITCHING QUIZ

1. Two Red Sox rookies won 20 or more games in the same year. Can you name them?
2. Who is the Red Sox rookie starting pitcher with the highest winning percentage?
3. The lowest ERA ever turned in by a Red Sox rookie is 1.82. It occurred in 1908. Do you know this sensational rookie?
4. The Red Sox rookie strikeout record is 144 and was set in 1913. Who was this brilliant strikeout artist?
5. In 1945 this fine Red Sox rookie hurler tossed five shutouts. Can you name him?

DID YOU KNOW that Boo Ferriss had the greatest season of all Red Sox rookies? In 1945 he completed 26 of 31 starts and won 21 of them. His ERA was a sharp 2.96.

DID YOU KNOW that Dick Radatz was the most outstanding Red Sox rookie relief pitcher? In 1962 he won nine and saved 24 with a brilliant 2.24 ERA in 62 appearances.

DID YOU KNOW that in 1912, with two rookie pitchers each winning 20 games, the Red Sox had their best season ever? They led the AL at 105–47 as Joe Wood also won 34 games.

Most Appearances

1901	George Winter	28
1906	Joe Harris	30
1907	Tex Pruiett	35
1908	Ed Cicotte	39
1912	Hugh Bedient	41
1913	Dutch Leonard	42
1928	Ed Morris	47
1958	Murray Wall	52
1962	**Dick Radatz**	***62**

Most Starts

1901	George Winter	28
1912	**Buck O'Brien**	**34**

Most Complete Games

1901	**George Winter**	**26**
1945	**Boo Ferriss**	**26**

Most Wins

1901	George Winter	16
1912	Hugh Bedient	20
	Buck O'Brien	20
1945	**Boo Ferriss**	**21**

Most Losses

1901	George Winter	12
1906	**Joe Harris**	**21**

Highest Winning Percentage

1901	George Winter	.571
1903	Norwood Gibson	.591
1909	Joe Wood	.611
1912	Hugh Bedient	.690
1914	Ernie Shore	.714
1969	**Mike Nagy**	**.857**

Lowest ERA

1901	George Winter	*2.80
1908	**Frank Arellanes**	**1.82**

Most Innings

1901	George Winter	241
1912	**Buck O'Brien**	**276**

Most Hits Allowed

1901	George Winter	234
1912	Buck O'Brien	237
1913	Dutch Leonard	245
1925	**Ted Wingfield**	**267**

Most Bases on Balls

1901	George Winter	66
1906	Joe Harris	67
1912	Buck O'Brien	90
1913	Dutch Leonard	94
1961	**Don Schwall**	**110**

Most Strikeouts

1901	George Winter	63
1903	Norwood Gibson	76
1906	Joe Harris	99
1912	Hugh Bedient	122
1913	**Dutch Leonard**	**144**

Most Shutouts

1901	George Winter	1
1903	Norwood Gibson	2
1907	Tex Pruiett	2
1908	Ed Cicotte	2
1909	Joe Wood	4
1945	**Boo Ferriss**	**5**

RELIEF PITCHING RECORDS

Most Appearances

1901	Fred Mitchell	4
1906	Ralph Glaze	9
1907	Tex Pruiett	*18
1915	Carl Mays	**32
1926	Tony Welzer	34
1944	Frank Barrett	36
1955	Tom Hurd	43
1958	Murray Wall	51
1962	**Dick Radatz**	***62**

Ted Williams: "I found you don't have to wear a necktie if you can hit."

Ed Linn on Ted Williams's retirement: "Now Boston knows how it feels when England lost India."

Most Wins

1901	Fred Mitchell	1
1903	Norwood Gibson	1
1906	Joe Harris	1
1908	Ed Cicotte	1
	Elmer Steele	1
1909	Joe Wood	2
1912	Hugh Bedient	*6
1944	Frank Barrett	7
1955	Tom Hurd	8
1958	Murray Wall	8
1962	**Dick Radatz**	**9**

Most Losses

1901–06	None	
1907	Tex Pruiett	1
1908	Ed Cicotte	2
1913	Dutch Leonard	5
1920	Benn Karr	**6
1944	Frank Barrett	6
1955	Tom Hurd	6
1958	**Murray Wall**	**8**

Most Saves

1901–05	None	
1906	Joe Harris	1
1907	Tex Pruiett	3
1915	Carl Mays	7
1944	Frank Barrett	8
1958	Murray Wall	10
1962	**Dick Radatz**	**24**

Most Wins Plus Saves

1901	Fred Mitchell	1
1903	Norwood Gibson	1
1906	Joe Harris	2
1907	Tex Pruiett	3
1909	Joe Wood	4
1912	Hugh Bedient	*8
1915	Carl Mays	12
1944	Frank Barrett	15
1958	Murray Wall	18
1962	**Dick Radatz**	****33**

Highest Winning Percentage (Minimum 10 Decisions)

1901–14	None	
1915	Carl Mays	.500
1944	Frank Barrett	.538
1955	Tom Hurd	.571
1962	**Dick Radatz**	**.600**

Lowest ERA

1915	Carl Mays	2.60
1962	**Dick Radatz**	**2.24**

Most Hits Allowed

1915	Carl Mays	119
1926	**Tony Welzer**	**167**

Most Bases on Balls

1915	Carl Mays	21
1920	Benn Karr	24
1924	Buster Ross	30
1926	**Tony Welzer**	**57**

Most Strikeouts

1915	Carl Mays	65
1962	**Dick Radatz**	**144**

Most Innings

1915	Carl Mays	132
1926	**Tony Welzer**	**141**

DID YOU KNOW that the Boudreau shift was first used on Ted Williams on July 14, 1946?

DID YOU KNOW that the Red Sox set a Major League record by scoring 17 runs in one inning on June 18, 1953?

DID YOU KNOW that the Red Sox offered $1 million for Herb Score?

RECORD HOLDERS LIST

1	George Winter	12	12	Ed Cicotte	4
2	Carl Mays	9	12	Tony Welzer	4
3	Dick Radatz	8	16	Boo Ferriss	3
4	Joe Harris	7	16	Fred Mitchell	3
5	Tex Pruiett	6	18	Benn Karr	2
5	Hugh Bedient	6	19	Ed Morris	1
5	Frank Barrett	6	19	Ernie Shore	1
5	Murray Wall	6	19	Mike Nagy	1
9	Buck O'Brien	5	19	Frank Arellanes	1
9	Dutch Leonard	5	19	Ted Wingfield	1
9	Norwood Gibson	5	19	Don Schwall	1
12	Joe Wood	4	19	Ralph Glaze	1
12	Tom Hurd	4	19	Elmer Steele	1
			19	Buster Ross	1

SUMMARY AND HIGHLIGHTS

George Winter was the only rookie starting pitcher in 1901, the club's first season. As a result he accumulated 12 records for others to shoot down. Winter was certainly an above-average pitcher, as is indicated by his career 2.87 ERA, but he was one of those hard-luck guys whose teams scored few runs while he was on the mound. In 8 years Winter's record showed 82 wins and 96 losses. As it turned out, his rookie year would be his most successful. He was traded to Detroit for cash, and after posting a dismal 1–5 mark with the Tigers, he called it a career.

Carl Mays won only one more game than he lost (6–5), but he put ten new records in the book. In 38 appearances the big righthander led the league in saves with seven. He worked 32 games in relief, which was a Major League record as well.

Mays ignored the sophomore jinx and won 18 games while settling down with a fine ERA of 2.39. He became a 20-game winner for the first time in 1917, when he won 22 and lost nine. He was almost as good in 1918, winning 21 and losing 13. In that year Mays led the league in complete games and shutouts. But in 1919 he suffered his first bad season, going 5–11, and was shipped to the Yankees for Allan Russell, Bob McGraw, and $40,000. When Babe Ruth rejoined Mays on the Yankees in 1920, Mays promptly won 26 games and did even better the following year, winning 27 times. After two average years he was sent to Cincinnati, where he proved to New York that he could still pitch by winning 20 and losing nine. After 15 years on the mound, Mays won 208 and lost 126 and had a fine 2.92 ERA. His winning percentage was .623, but he never made it to the Hall of Fame even though there are some pitchers there with worse credentials.

The Red Sox did not benefit from Allan Russell, who was a losing pitcher for 3 years (18–24) before being traded off. Bob McGraw was sent back to the Yankees after going 0–2 in ten games. The only gain Boston made was the $40,000 cash.

The saddest day of Carl Mays's career came in 1920, when he beaned Cleveland shortstop Ray Chapman, who died as a result of the pitch. Mays was accused of deliberately throwing at Chapman, but Chapman was known for crowding the plate, and some people say the pitch that hit him was actually in the strike zone.

Hugh Bedient and Buck O'Brien made American League history in 1912,

DICK RADATZ

RECORD PROFILE
DICK RADATZ
ROOKIE PITCHING RECORDS

1962			
	Most Appearances	62	NEVER BROKEN
	Most Relief Appearances	62	NEVER BROKEN
	Most Relief Wins	9	NEVER BROKEN
	Most Saves	24	NEVER BROKEN
	Most Wins Plus Saves	33	NEVER BROKEN
	Highest Winning Percentage	.600	NEVER BROKEN
	Lowest ERA	2.24	NEVER BROKEN
	Most Strikeouts	144	NEVER BROKEN

when they became the first and only pair of rookies on one team to win 20 or more games each. They were also the first Boston rookies to win 20 games and strike out more than 100 batters.

The double 20-game winners tied a Major League record set way back in 1887, when Ed Seward and Gus Weyhing of Philadelphia first accomplished the amazing feat. This took place in the old American Association, which was considered a "major league" in those days. Seward's record was 25–25, and Weyhing won 26 and lost 28. This rare happening took place for the first time in the National League in 1903. Henry Schmidt won 21 and lost 13, and Oscar Jones won 20 and lost 16 while playing for Brooklyn.

In 1937 Milkman Jim Turner and Lou Fette of the Boston Braves turned the trick for the last time in the National League. Turner, who would later be a fine pitcher and coach for the New York Yankees, won 20 and lost 11, while Fette was 20–10.

Buck O'Brien is also famous for starting the most games and pitching the most innings of any Red Sox rookie. These records have never been broken. But O'Brien's success was short-lived, as he won only four games while losing nine the following year before being traded to Chicago, where he went 0–2 and was out of the game forever.

Boo Ferriss's 21 wins in 1945 represents the most of any rookie in Red Sox history. The following year he had one of the best seasons of any pitcher in baseball. He won 25 times with only six losses and had a league-leading .806 winning percentage. His efforts were a major contribution toward winning the pennant, and he even tossed a shutout in his first World Series game, against the Cardinals. However, Ferriss's luck ran out in the seventh game of that series, when he was removed after pitching four and a third innings with his team behind.

The Red Sox tied the score before losing that game and the series 4–3. Ferriss developed arm trouble, and after going 12–11 in 1947 and 7–3 in 1948, he had no decisions in 1949 and 1950 before realizing that his career was over.

Another pitcher with outstanding potential was Mike Nagy in 1969. After setting a still-standing winning percentage record of .857, in which he won 12 and lost two, the 6' 3" righthander would win only seven while losing eight during the next three seasons. He was traded for Lance Clemens in 1973 and was out of baseball after going 1–1 in 1974. (Clemens only won one game for Boston, and his career also ended in 1974.)

Frank Arellanes qualified as a rookie by pitching more than the required 50 innings (79⅓), and in his 11 outings spun a cool 1.82 ERA, which represents a still-standing record since 1908. Arellanes won 16 while dropping 12 in his second year but became ineffective in 1910, which proved to be his last year in the Major Leagues.

The story of Red Ruffing is quite intriguing. As a rookie in 1925 this outstanding hitting pitcher had a losing season of 9–18. He continued to have five more losing seasons, the worst of which were 10–25 in 1928 and

9–22 in 1929. His 25 losses would be the most of any pitcher in Red Sox history.

On May 6, 1930, Ruffing was traded to the New York Yankees (hard to believe that any team would want him) for Cedric Durst and $50,000. But Ruffing did a complete turnaround, perhaps taking a liking to the deep pastures of Yankee Stadium, and became one of the best pitchers in Yankee history. Four times he won 20 or more games, and in his 15 years with the Bronx Bombers he won 231 games while losing 125. He had been 39–96 with the Red Sox! Ruffing's fine work with the Yankees earned him a berth in the Hall of Fame.

In 1909 Smokey Joe Wood tossed four shutouts, setting a new record on his way to winning 11 games. He seemed to have stardom written all over him but only had a mediocre year in 1910, going 12–13. The hard-throwing pitcher settled down to a fine season in 1911 by winning 23 and dropping 17 and then astounded the baseball world in 1912 by winning 34 games with only 5 losses. He was a league leader in winning percentage (.872) and complete games (35), and his ten shutouts are still a club record.

However, Smokey Joe could crank up his arm for only 11 wins in 1913 and nine in 1914 before having a good year in 1915 with 15 wins. The Red Sox lost faith in him, though, and off to Cleveland he went for $15,000. The front office was right in this case, as Joe Wood would not win a single game for Cleveland for the next 3 years. He only appeared in seven games, with one loss. He was considered "dead wood" at the age of 31.

Dick "The Monster" Radatz's eight records represent the third most of Boston rookies, and he put in three fine seasons of relief work. During that span the big righthander won 40, lost 21, and saved 78 before suffering losing seasons in 1965 and 1966. Radatz ended his career pitching for Cleveland, Chicago, and Montreal, but he had little left after giving so much to the Red Sox.

When Dutch Leonard donned the Red Sox uniform for the first time in 1913, he won 14 times but lost 16 times. But this fine pitcher steadily improved, shattering the sophomore jinx in 1914 with 19 wins and only five defeats, then was 15–7 in 1915 and 18–12 in 1916. Leonard had average success in 1917 and 1918 before being traded to Detroit for cash. In his last 5 years, with Detroit, he won 49 and lost 49.

The most losses ever recorded by a Boston rookie occurred in 1906, when Joe Harris took it on the chin 21 times. He won only two games, but the Red Sox saw something in him that they liked and gave him another chance in 1907. They finally gave up on him after Harris lost seven games in a row.

It is said that you win some and lose some, but the Red Sox have given up many more good players than they have traded for. Another case is that of pitcher Ed Cicotte. He was only fair with Boston, with a 51–46 mark, before he was traded to Chicago for cash. He showed Boston they had given up on him too soon, as he had winning seasons of 28, 29, and 21 games. In all he won 156 and lost 102 for Chicago. Cicotte was infamous for his part in fixing the 1919 World Series. Although it is well documented that Cicotte was involved, he also did very little to lose games. Cicotte started the first game of the World Series and allowed one run in 3.2 innings. He pitched a five-hitter and lost a 2–0 shutout in game four and pitched a seven-hitter and won 4–1 in game seven, and Cincinnati won the eight-game series five games to three. Cicotte did not pitch any part of the final game. When asked why he agreed to fixing the games, he is quoted as saying, "I did it for my kids."

CHAPTER VI

ROOKIE FIELDING RECORDS

FIELDING QUIZ

1. In 1955, this weak-hitting but slick-fielding first baseman set a Red Sox fielding percentage record that has never been broken. Name him.
2. In 1961 a sure-handed, smooth-fielding second baseman broke a 60-year-old Red Sox record in putouts. Who is he?
3. Can you name the rookie catcher who set three records in 1972?
4. What leftfielder erased Carl Yastrzemski's Red Sox record for fewest errors in left field?
5. One record Ted Williams is not proud of is how many errors he made as a rookie. How many did he make?

DID YOU KNOW that Jim Rice is the only Red Sox rookie outfielder to go through a season without making an error? The 90 games he played, though, did not qualify him for a record.

DID YOU KNOW that no Red Sox rookie leftfielder has ever improved upon Duffy Lewis's assists and double play records of 1910?

DID YOU KNOW that Ted Williams chased down more fly balls than any rookie rightfielder in Boston history?

FIRST BASE

Most Putouts
1901–04	No Rookies	
1905	Moose Grimshaw	768
1935	**Babe Dahlgren**	**1,433**

Most Assists
1901–04	No Rookies	
1905	Moose Grimshaw	35
1935	Babe Dahlgren	69
1966	**George Scott**	**112**

Most Errors
1905	Moose Grimshaw	16
1935	**Babe Dahlgren**	**18**

Fewest Errors
1901–04	No Rookies	
1905	Moose Grimshaw	16
1942	Tony Lupien	9
1948	Billy Goodman	8
1955	**Norm Zauchin**	**6**

Most Double Plays
1901–04	No Rookies	
1905	Moose Grimshaw	35
1935	Babe Dahlgren	109
1950	**Walt Dropo**	**147**

Most Chances Per Game
1901–04	No Rookies	
1905	**Moose Grimshaw**	**11.1**

Most Total Chances
1901–04	No Rookies	
1905	Moose Grimshaw	819
1935	**Babe Dahlgren**	**1,520**

Highest Fielding Percentage
1901–04	No Rookies	
1905	Moose Grimshaw	.980
1935	Babe Dahlgren	.988
1942	Tony Lupien	.992
1948	Billy Goodman	.993
1955	**Norm Zauchin**	**.995**

* American League Record
** Major League Record
*** Unbroken Major League Record

SECOND BASE

Most Putouts
1901	Hobe Ferris	*359
1961	**Chuck Schilling**	***397**

Most Assists
1901	Hobe Ferris	*450

Most Errors
1901	Hobe Ferris	*61

Fewest Errors
1901	Hobe Ferris	61
1908	Amby McConnell	38
1910	Larry Gardner	32
1926	Bill Regan	24
1961	**Chuck Schilling**	**8**

Most Double Plays
1901	Hobe Ferris	**68
1932	Marv Olson	68
1961	**Chuck Schilling**	***121**

Most Chances Per Game
1901	Hobe Ferris	*6.3
1926	**Bill Regan**	**6.4**

Most Total Chances
1901	Hobe Ferris	770
1961	**Chuck Schilling**	**854**

Highest Fielding Percentage
1901	Hobe Ferris	.930
1908	Amby McConnell	.939
1910	Larry Gardner	.944
1926	Bill Regan	.963
1961	**Chuck Schilling**	***.991

SHORTSTOP

Most Putouts
1901	Freddy Parent	260
1907	Heinie Wagner	283
1914	**Everett Scott**	**324**

Most Assists
1901	Freddy Parent	*446
1942	**Johnny Pesky**	**465**

Most Errors
1901 Freddy Parent   63

Fewest Errors
1901 Freddy Parent   *63
1907 Heinie Wagner   50
1914 Everett Scott   39
1942 Johnny Pesky   37
1953 Milt Bolling   23

Most Double Plays
1901 Freddy Parent   *52
1942 Johnny Pesky   94
1956 Don Buddin   98

Most Chances Per Game
1901 Freddy Parent   *5.6
1907 Heinie Wagner   6.6

Most Total Chances
1901 Freddy Parent   *769
1914 Everett Scott   771
1942 Johnny Pesky   882

Highest Fielding Percentage
1901 Freddy Parent   .918
1907 Heinie Wagner   .931
1914 Everett Scott   **.949
1942 Johnny Pesky   .955
1953 Milt Bolling   .956

Fewest Errors
1901–05   No Rookies
1906 Red Morgan   41
1939 Jim Tabor   40
1957 Frank Malzone   25

Most Double Plays
1901–05   No Rookies
1906 Red Morgan   8
1908 Harry Lord   13
1939 Jim Tabor   *32

Most Chances Per Game
1901–05   No Rookies
1906 Red Morgan   3.5
1908 Harry Lord   3.5
1939 Jim Tabor   3.5
1957 Frank Malzone   3.6

Most Total Chances
1901–05   No Rookies
1906 Red Morgan   306
1908 Harry Lord   499
1939 Jim Tabor   522
1957 Frank Malzone   546

Highest Fielding Percentage
1906 Red Morgan   .866
1908 Harry Lord   .906
1939 Jim Tabor   .923
1957 Frank Malzone   .954

THIRD BASE

Most Putouts
1901–05   No Rookies
1906 Red Morgan   126
1908 Harry Lord   181

Most Assists
1901–05   No Rookies
1906 Red Morgan   139
1908 Harry Lord   271
1939 Jim Tabor   338
1957 Frank Malzone   370

Most Errors
1901–05   No Rookies
1906 Red Morgan   41
1908 Harry Lord   47

CATCHING

Most Putouts
1901–05   No Rookies
1906 Charlie Armbruster   262
1942 Bill Conroy   324
1943 Roy Partee   349
1952 Sammy White   464
1961 John Pagliaroni   586
1966 Mike Ryan   685
1972 Carlton Fisk   *846

Harry Hooper on Babe Ruth: "I saw a man transformed from a human being into something pretty close to a god."

Most Assists

1901–05	No Rookies	
1906	**Charlie Armbruster**	**99**

Most Errors

1906	**Charlie Armbruster**	**17**

Fewest Errors

1901–05	No Rookies	
1906	Charlie Armbruster	17
1943	Roy Partee	7
1966	**Mike Ryan**	**6**

Most Double Plays

1901–05	No Rookies	
1906	Charlie Armbruster	6
1942	Bill Conroy	6
1943	**Roy Partee**	**11**

Most Chances Per Game

1901–05	No Rookies	
1906	Charlie Armbruster	5.7
1961	John Pagliaroni	5.9
1966	Mike Ryan	6.5
1972	**Carlton Fisk**	***7.1**

Most Total Chances

1901–05	No Rookies	
1906	Charlie Armbruster	378
1943	Roy Partee	413
1952	Sammy White	532
1961	John Pagliaroni	635
1966	Mike Ryan	741
1972	**Carlton Fisk**	***933**

Highest Fielding Percentage

1901–05	No Rookies	
1906	Charlie Armbruster	.955
1943	Roy Partee	.983
1961	John Pagliaroni	.984
1966	**Mike Ryan**	**.992**

LEFT FIELD

Most Putouts

1901	No Rookies	
1902	Pat Dougherty	*170
1910	Duffy Lewis	261
1929	**Russ Scarritt**	**302**

Most Assists

1901	No Rookies	
1902	Pat Dougherty	*8
1910	**Duffy Lewis**	***28**

Most Errors

1901	No Rookies	
1902	**Pat Dougherty**	***20**

Fewest Errors

1901	No Rookies	
1902	Pat Dougherty	20
1906	John Hoey	15
1961	Carl Yastrzemski	10
1970	**Billy Conigliaro**	**7**

Most Double Plays

1901	No Rookies	
1902	Pat Dougherty	*1
1910	**Duffy Lewis**	****9**

Most Chances Per Game

1901	No Rookies	
1902	Pat Dougherty	*1.9
1906	John Hoey	1.9
1910	Duffy Lewis	2.1
1929	**Russ Scarritt**	**2.3**

Most Total Chances

1901	No Rookies	
1902	Pat Dougherty	*198
1910	Duffy Lewis	306
1929	**Russ Scarritt**	**337**

Highest Fielding Percentage

1901	No Rookies	
1902	Pat Dougherty	.899
1906	John Hoey	.915
1910	Duffy Lewis	.944
1929	Russ Scarritt	.944
1961	Carl Yastrzemski	.963
1970	**Billy Conigliaro**	**.968**

CENTER FIELD

Most Putouts

1901–06	No Rookies	
1907	Denny Sullivan	*296
1930	**Tommy Oliver**	****477**

Most Assists

1901–06	No Rookies	
1907	Denny Sullivan	16

Most Errors

1901–06	No Rookies	
1907	Denny Sullivan	8

Fewest Errors

1901–06	No Rookies	
1907	Denny Sullivan	8
1953	Tommy Umphlett	7
1967	Reggie Smith	7
1987	Ellis Burks	4

Most Double Plays

1901–06	No Rookies	
1907	Denny Sullivan	3
1967	Reggie Smith	3

Most Chances Per Game

1901–06	No Rookies	
1907	Denny Sullivan	2.2
1930	Tommy Oliver	*3.2
1967	Reggie Smith	*3.2

Most Total Chances

1901–06	No Rookies	
1907	Denny Sullivan	320
1930	Tommy Oliver	***495

Highest Fielding Percentage

1901–06	No Rookies	
1907	Denny Sullivan	**.975
1930	Tommy Oliver	*.982
1953	Tommy Umphlett	.983
1967	Reggie Smith	.983
1975	Fred Lynn	.983
1987	Ellis Burks	.988

RIGHT FIELD

Most Putouts

1901–08	No Rookies	
1909	Harry Hooper	124
1924	Ike Boone	189
1928	Doug Taitt	*251
1939	Ted Williams	*318

Most Assists

1901–08	No Rookies	
1909	Harry Hooper	14
1924	Ike Boone	17
1928	Doug Taitt	19

Most Errors

1901–08	No Rookies	
1909	Harry Hooper	7
1928	Doug Taitt	7
1939	Ted Williams	19

Fewest Errors

1901–08	No Rookies	
1909	Harry Hooper	7
1924	Ike Boone	5
1947	Sam Mele	2

Most Double Plays

1901–08	No Rookies	
1909	Harry Hooper	3
1924	Ike Boone	3
1928	Doug Taitt	*8

Most Chances Per Game

1901–08	No Rookies	
1909	Harry Hooper	1.7
1924	Ike Boone	1.7
1928	Doug Taitt	2.0
1939	Ted Williams	*2.3
1940	Dom DiMaggio	2.8

Most Total Chances

1901–08	No Rookies	
1909	Harry Hooper	145
1924	Ike Boone	211
1928	Doug Taitt	277
1939	Ted Williams	*348

Highest Fielding Percentage

1901–08	No Rookies	
1909	Harry Hooper	.952
1924	Ike Boone	*.976
1940	Dom DiMaggio	.977
1947	Sam Mele	***.992

DID YOU KNOW that Joe Cronin was the first former player to become president of either league?

RECORD HOLDERS LIST

1	Harry Hooper	8
1	Denny Sullivan	8
1	Moose Grimshaw	8
1	Hobe Ferris	8
1	Freddy Parent	8
1	Charlie Armbruster	8
1	Red Morgan	8
1	Pat Dougherty	8
9	Harry Lord	7
9	Ike Boone	7
11	Doug Taitt	6
11	Duffy Lewis	6
11	Jim Tabor	6
11	Babe Dahlgren	6
15	Roy Partee	5
15	Frank Malzone	5
15	Mike Ryan	5
15	Johnny Pesky	5
15	Chuck Schilling	5
20	John Pagliaroni	4
20	Heinie Wagner	4
20	Ted Williams	4
20	Russ Scarritt	4
20	Reggie Smith	4
20	Everett Scott	4
20	Tommy Oliver	4
27	John Hoey	3
27	Bill Regan	3
27	Carlton Fisk	3
30	Dom DiMaggio	2
30	Bill Conroy	2
30	Sam Mele	2
30	Tony Lupien	2
30	Billy Goodman	2
30	Amby McConnell	2
30	Larry Gardner	2
30	Sammy White	2
30	Milt Bolling	2
30	Carl Yastrzemski	2
30	Billy Conigliaro	2
30	Ellis Burks	2
42	Tommy Umphlett	1
42	Fred Lynn	1
42	George Scott	1
42	Walt Dropo	1
42	Norm Zauchin	1
42	Marv Olson	1
42	Don Buddin	1

SUMMARY AND HIGHLIGHTS

The most active and impressive rookie first baseman was Dahlgren in 1935. Although he established six rookie fielding records and three of them remain unbroken, Dahlgren is most famous for being traded to the Yankees and being Lou Gehrig's replacement in 1939. Dahlgren batted .263 his freshman season, getting 138 hits. He played only 16 games for Boston in 1936 and was traded for cash in 1937, but he played only one game for the Yankees that year. In his 12-year career Dahlgren would be traded eight times. After playing 29 games for the Yankees in 1938 (Gehrig was still playing), Babe took over on that sorrowful day in 1939 when Lou Gehrig could play no more. He batted only .235 but did slam 15 home runs. He hit 12 homers in 1940 and improved his average to .264, but he began a heavy traveling schedule in 1941 that took him to the Braves and Cubs and then to the Cardinals and Dodgers in 1942, to the Phillies in 1943 and to the Pirates in 1944 and 1945. He ended his career with the St. Louis Browns in the American League in 1946. Dahlgren's best season was with the Pirates in 1944, when he hit 12 home runs and batted .289. His lifetime batting average was .261.

This writer had the privilege of being a teammate of Chuck Schilling in his college days at Manhattan College in 1957. Schilling went on to become the greatest Red Sox rookie second baseman in 1961. Schilling's 397 put-outs broke a 60-year-old record set by Hobe Ferris in the first year of the club's existence, in 1901.

The errors record began with 61 in 1901, and many players had reduced the mark to 24 by 1926. The 1926 record was extremely difficult to break, yet Chuck Schilling shattered it by making only eight errors. This produced a record fielding percentage of .991, which also was a Major League record.

Schilling was not only a slick fielder in picking up ground balls, but he was a master at turning the double play. The best previous record was 68 double plays, established in 1901 and then tied in 1932. Schilling improved this record by adding 53 more twin killings for a total of 121. In all the smooth-fielding second sacker tallied 854 total chances, which represents five records that still remain unbroken.

DUFFY LEWIS

RECORD PROFILE
DUFFY LEWIS
ROOKIE FIELDING RECORDS
LEFT FIELD

1910	Most Putouts	261	19 years before broken
	Most Assists	28	**NEVER BROKEN**
	Most Double Plays	9	**NEVER BROKEN**
	Most Chances Per Game	2.1	19 years before broken
	Most Total Chances	306	19 years before broken
	Highest Fielding Percentage	.944	19 years before broken

Everett Scott would get the vote for having the best hands at shortstop, as is indicated by his .949 fielding average of 1914. The highest fielding average belongs to Milt Bolling, but his .956 average is only seven points higher than Scott's—not much better, given his better equipment.

Scott did not hit very much, but he was considered one of the best-fielding shortstops in the game. He would have to be exceptional to stay in the big leagues, with batting averages of .201, .232, .241, and .221. In 1919 he finally began to hit respectably for the Red Sox, and he batted .278, .269, and .262 before being traded to the Yankees in 1922.

Scott played a big role in helping the Yankees to win pennants in 1922 and 1923. He led the league in assists and fielding percentage in 1922 and in fielding percentage again in 1923. That's exactly what the Yankees needed—good fielding, to go along with their power offense. Prior to going to the Yankees, Scott had led the league in fielding percentage 6 years in a row, and when he added two more fielding percentage crowns with the Yankees, it marked the first and only time any defensive player had led the league in fielding percentage 8 years in a row.

When Scott was traded to the Yankees, it was a package deal in which Boston gave up Scott, Joe Bush, and Sad Sam Jones in exchange for Roger Peckinpaugh, Jack Quinn, Rip Collins, and Bill Piercy. A quick check of the records shows that the Yankees got the best of this trade by far.

Prior to the arrival of Wade Boggs, the most outstanding Red Sox third baseman was Frank Malzone. Malzone was born in the Bronx, not far from Yankee Stadium, and got his first shot with Boston in 1955, when he played in six games. The following season he played in 27 games, and he did not become a regular until 1957. In that year he played in 153 games and batted a strong .292 with 15 home runs. It was a year in which he would become the most active rookie third baseman in Red Sox history. But even more amazing is the fact that he led the league in *every* fielding category! In the history of baseball that is about as rare as a no-hitter.

In addition to being a fine fielder, Malzone was a very good hitter. After batting .292 in his first full season, he batted over .290 two more times and ended his 12-year career with a .274 batting average and 133 home runs.

Carlton Fisk was the most exciting rookie catcher, and he also turned out to be the club's greatest catcher all-around. There may have been better defensive catchers than "Pudge," as the 6' 3" 200-pounder is called. But his lifetime batting average and more than 230 home runs easily rate him as the number-one Boston catcher.

Fisk still has three unbroken rookie fielding records to his credit in a year he batted .293. Twice he batted over .300, with a high of .331 in 1975. Twice he had seasons of 26 home runs. After 11 fine years with Boston, Fisk became a free agent and accepted an offer from the White Sox, where he is still active.

The Red Sox have had some outstanding leftfielders. Duffy Lewis was the first full-timer, and he put in eight solid seasons (1910–17). The club did not have any rookies who could break Lewis's records until Russ Scarritt came along in 1929. Scarritt set three new marks and tied one and is still the club leader in three departments. After batting a fine .294 in his first season, he hit .289 the following year. But he played only ten games in 1931 and then was traded to the Phillies in 1932, where his career ended after 11 games.

So outstanding were the accomplishments of Lewis and Scarritt that no rookie left field fielding record was broken until Carl Yastrzemski took on the Green Monster in 1961. Yaz set a new record for fewest errors and improved the fielding percentage mark to .963.

The Red Sox had only one Hall of Famer in center field, and that was Tris Speaker. But Speaker had too many at bats in brief appearances in 1907 and 1908 to qualify for rookie honors in 1909.

Dom DiMaggio, who was one of Boston's best centerfielders, began his career in right field. Tommy Oliver and Reggie Smith also did some fine work in the main pasture. Present-day star Ellis Burks set a new record for fewest errors and highest fielding percentage, and he has the potential to be one of the best.

Harry Hooper was Boston's first superstar in right field, and he became a Hall of Famer in 1971 after 12 years with the team.

Before switching to left field, Ted Williams spent his rookie season as a rightfielder and to this date still has the most putouts, total chances, and errors of any rookie rightfielder.

CHAPTER VII

CAREER BATTING RECORDS

BATTING QUIZ

1. Who was the first player to have a 10-year career with the Red Sox?
2. Only one Red Sox player has had a career that spanned more than 20 years. Do you know him?
3. This Hall of Famer was the first Red Sox player to come to bat 5,000 times. Name him.
4. The all-time Red Sox triples record is 130. Can you name the player who set it?
5. Only one Red Sox player has over 5,000 total bases. Who is he?

DID YOU KNOW that Carl Yastrzemski's 11 unbroken records are the most of any Red Sox player?

DID YOU KNOW that Bobby Doerr was the first player to complete a 14-year career? He retired with the most games played, at bats, hits, singles, doubles, home runs, extra base hits, total bases, runs scored, and RBIs.

DID YOU KNOW that Tris Speaker was the first Red Sox player to appear in 1,000 games, get more than 1,300 hits, hit 100 triples, and score more than 700 runs?

Most Years

1901–03	Harry Gleason	3
1902–04	Pat Dougherty	3
1902–05	Candy LaChance	4
1901–06	Chick Stahl	*6
1901–07	Buck Freeman	*7
	Hobe Ferris	*7
	Freddy Parent	*7
1901–08	Lou Criger	*8
1907–15	Tris Speaker	9
1908–17	Larry Gardner	10
1906–18	Heinie Wagner	11
1909–20	Harry Hooper	12
1937–51	Bobby Doerr	14
1939–60	Ted Williams	19
1961–83	**Carl Yastrzemski**	**23**

Most Games

1901–03	Harry Gleason	78
1902–04	Pat Dougherty	296
1902–05	Candy LaChance	*448
1901–06	Chick Stahl	*781
1901–07	Hobe Ferris	*990
1907–15	Tris Speaker	1,065
1910–17	Duffy Lewis	1,184
1909–20	Harry Hooper	1,646
1937–51	Bobby Doerr	1,865
1939–60	Ted Williams	2,292
1961–83	**Carl Yastrzemski**	**3,308**

Most At Bats

1901–03	Harry Gleason	254
1902–04	Pat Dougherty	1,124
1902–05	Candy LaChance	*1,677
1901–06	Chick Stahl	*3,004
1901–07	Freddy Parent	*3,846
1907–15	Tris Speaker	3,947
1909–20	Harry Hooper	6,270
1937–51	Bobby Doerr	7,093
1939–60	Ted Williams	7,706
1961–83	**Carl Yastrzemksi**	**11,988**

Most Hits

1901–03	Harry Gleason	57
1902–04	Pat Dougherty	394
1902–05	Candy LaChance	*421
1901–06	Chick Stahl	*877
1901–07	Freddy Parent	*1,051
1907–15	Tris Speaker	1,328
1909–20	Harry Hooper	1,707
1937–51	Bobby Doerr	2,042
1939–60	Ted Williams	2,654
1961–83	**Carl Yastrzemksi**	**3,419**

Most Singles

1901–03	Harry Gleason	44
1902–04	Pat Dougherty	328
1902–05	Candy LaChance	*343
1901–06	Chick Stahl	*682
1901–07	Freddy Parent	813
1907–15	Tris Speaker	941
1909–20	Harry Hooper	1,301
1937–51	Bobby Doerr	1,349
1939–60	Ted Williams	1,537
1961–83	**Carl Yastrzemksi**	**2,262**

Most Doubles

1901–03	Harry Gleason	6
1902–04	Pat Dougherty	39
1902–05	Candy LaChance	55
1901–06	Chick Stahl	*122
1901–07	Jimmy Collins	171
1907–15	Tris Speaker	241
1910–17	Duffy Lewis	254
1935–45	Joe Cronin	270
1937–51	Bobby Doerr	381
1939–60	Ted Williams	525
1961–83	**Carl Yastrzemksi**	**646**

Most Triples

1901–03	Harry Gleason	5
1902–04	Pat Dougherty	21
1901–06	Chick Stahl	*62
1901–07	Buck Freeman	*90
1907–15	Tris Speaker	107
1909–20	**Harry Hooper**	**130**

DID YOU KNOW that Joe Cronin hit into a triple play by lining a ball off the third baseman's head (1935)?

Most Home Runs

1901–03	Harry Gleason	2
1902–04	Pat Dougherty	6
1902–05	Candy LaChance	8
1901–06	Chick Stahl	*17
1901–07	Buck Freeman	*48
1935–45	Joe Cronin	119
1936–42	Jimmy Foxx	217
1937–51	Bobby Doerr	223
1939–60	**Ted Williams**	**521**

Highest Home Run Percentage

1901–03	Harry Gleason	0.1
1902–04	Pat Dougherty	0.2
1902–05	Candy LaChance	0.3
1901–06	Chick Stahl	0.5
1901–07	Buck Freeman	*1.5
1915–19	Babe Ruth	3.6
1936–42	Jimmy Foxx	6.7
1939–60	**Ted Williams**	**6.8**

Most Grand Slams

1939–60	Ted Williams	17

Most Extra Base Hits

1901–03	Harry Gleason	13
1902–04	Pat Dougherty	66
1902–05	Candy LaChance	78
1901–06	Chick Stahl	*201
1901–07	Buck Freeman	*296
1907–15	Tris Speaker	387
1909–20	Harry Hooper	406
1936–42	Jimmy Foxx	439
1937–51	Bobby Doerr	693
1939–60	Ted Williams	1,117
1961–83	**Carl Yastrzemski**	**1,157**

Most Total Bases

1901–03	Harry Gleason	79
1902–04	Pat Dougherty	493
1902–05	Candy LaChance	*530
1901–06	Chick Stahl	*1,174
1901–07	Buck Freeman	*1,264
1907–15	Tris Speaker	1,900
1909–20	Harry Hooper	2,303
1937–51	Bobby Doerr	3,270
1939–60	Ted Williams	4,884
1961–83	**Carl Yastrzemski**	**5,539**

Most Runs

1901–03	Harry Gleason	33
1902–04	Pat Dougherty	223
1901–06	Chick Stahl	*465
1901–07	Freddy Parent	519
1907–15	Tris Speaker	703
1909–20	Harry Hooper	988
1937–51	Bobby Doerr	1,094
1939–60	Ted Williams	1,798
1961–83	**Carl Yastrzemski**	**1,816**

Most RBIs

1901–03	Harry Gleason	27
1902–04	Pat Dougherty	101
1902–05	Candy LaChance	*161
1901–06	Chick Stahl	*339
1901–07	Buck Freeman	*504
1907–15	Tris Speaker	570
1910–17	Duffy Lewis	629
1936–42	Jimmy Foxx	774
1937–51	Bobby Doerr	1,247
1939–60	Ted Williams	1,839
1961–83	**Carl Yastrzemski**	**1,844**

Most Bases on Balls

1901–03	Harry Gleason	10
1902–04	Pat Dougherty	85
1901–06	Chick Stahl	*280
1907–15	Tris Speaker	459
1909–20	Harry Hooper	826
1939–60	**Ted Williams**	**2,018**

Most Strikeouts

1901–12	Statistics Not Kept	
1913–15	Tris Speaker	61
1910–17	Duffy Lewis	269
1909–20	Harry Hooper	289
1936–42	Jimmy Foxx	553
1937–51	Bobby Doerr	608
1939–60	Ted Williams	709
1963–76	Rico Petrocelli	926
1961–83	**Carl Yastrzemski**	**1,393**

DID YOU KNOW that Red Sox players tried to prevent Babe Ruth from taking batting practice by sawing his bats in half?

Most Stolen Bases

1901–03	Harry Gleason	7
1902–04	Pat Dougherty	62
1901–06	Chick Stahl	105
1901–07	Freddy Parent	129
1907–15	Tris Speaker	266
1909–20	Harry Hooper	300

Highest Batting Average (Minimum 5 Years)

1901–06	Chick Stahl	.290
1907–15	Tris Speaker	.340
1939–60	Ted Williams	.344
1982–88	**Wade Boggs**	**.354**

Highest Slugging Percentage (Minimum 5 Years)

1901–06	Chick Stahl	.389
1901–07	Buck Freeman	*.436
1907–15	Tris Speaker	.488
1915–19	Babe Ruth	.535
1936–42	Jimmy Foxx	.627
1939–60	**Ted Williams**	**.634**

Most Pinch At Bats

1901–03	Harry Gleason	12
1905–07	Moose Grimshaw	25
1908–11	Jack Thoney	31
1915–17	Chick Shorten	42
1920–23	Mike Menosky	44
1925–26	Roy Carlyle	46
1925–32	Jack Rothrock	88
1935–45	Joe Cronin	100
1952–60	Gene Stephens	113
1961–65	Russ Nixon	129
1964–69	**Dalton Jones**	**204**

Most Pinch Hits

1901–03	Harry Gleason	*3
1901–07	Buck Freeman	*6
1906–08	John Hoey	9
1920–23	Mike Menosky	13
1921–25	Shano Collins	13
1925–26	Roy Carlyle	18
1925–32	Jack Rothrock	27
1935–45	Joe Cronin	29
1939–60	Ted Williams	33
1961–65	Russ Nixon	40
1964–69	**Dalton Jones**	**55**

Highest Pinch Batting Average (Minimum 50 At Bats)

1925–32	Jack Rothrock	.307
1961–65	**Russ Nixon**	**.310**

RECORD HOLDERS LIST

1	Ted Williams	18
2	Chick Stahl	17
2	Harry Gleason	17
4	Tris Speaker	16
5	Pat Dougherty	15
6	Harry Hooper	12
6	Bobby Doerr	12
8	Carl Yastrzemski	11
8	Candy LaChance	11
10	Buck Freeman	9
11	Jimmy Foxx	6
12	Duffy Lewis	5
12	Freddy Parent	5
14	Joe Cronin	3
14	Jack Rothrock	3
14	Russ Nixon	3
17	Hobe Ferris	2
17	Babe Ruth	2
17	Mike Menosky	2
17	Roy Carlyle	2
17	Dalton Jones	2
22	John Hoey	1
22	Rico Petrocelli	1
22	Jimmy Collins	1
22	Moose Grimshaw	1
22	Jack Thoney	1
22	Chick Shorten	1
22	Gene Stephens	1
22	Shano Collins	1
22	Lou Criger	1
22	Larry Gardner	1
22	Heinie Wagner	1

DID YOU KNOW that although the Red Sox always loaded up with righthanded hitters to take advantage of the left field wall, the 18 league batting crowns won by Red Sox players after 1941 were all by lefthanders? (Ted Williams, six; Carl Yastrzemski, three; Pete Runnells, two; Billy Goodman, one; Fred Lynn, one; and Wade Boggs, five.)

SUMMARY AND HIGHLIGHTS

It is no surprise that Ted Williams is at the top of the career record holders list. He is without doubt the greatest player in Red Sox history. Ponder this: In his 19-year career, the smooth-swinging lefty accumulated 84 records! They consist of eight American League (three unbroken), three Major League (three unbroken), 17 All-Star game (nine unbroken), one World Series (unbroken), and 55 Boston club records (25 unbroken)!

The Splendid Splinter led the league a remarkable 44 times in various batting categories. Twice he led in doubles, he was a four-time home run champion, and five times he had the highest home run percentage. Six times he scored the most runs, and four times he was the RBI king.

His eyes were so keen that it has been said that if he let a pitch go by, the umpires knew it had to have been a ball. His awareness of the strike zone was so fantastic that he led the league in bases on balls eight times! Swinging at good pitches led the Thumper to six batting titles and nine slugging crowns.

Many experts say that Ted Williams was the greatest hitter of them all. It is true that Ty Cobb's lifetime batting average of .367 might seem superior to Ted's .344. But when the eras of both players are examined, most would agree that Williams's average was comparable to Cobb's. The reasoning is that little relief pitching existed in the Cobb era (1905–28), but during the Williams era (1939–1960), relief pitching had become a major factor in the game. Ty Cobb did not have to face as many tough lefthanded relief pitchers, and it is also important to note that hitting is easier off tiring pitchers, as was the situation when little relief pitching existed.

It is unfair to compare the home run power of the two greats because Cobb played most of his career in the dead-ball era. Yet it is also clear that Ted Williams had more power.

There are some who even go so far as to say that Ted Williams was the greatest home run hitter of all time. And where does that leave Babe Ruth and Hank Aaron? The arguments go like this: Babe Ruth had the advantage of the friendly confines of Yankee Stadium (344 feet) compared to the 380-foot distance in right field at Fenway Park. Ruth also did not have to face as many lefthanded relief pitchers in his day, and he too had the advantage of facing tiring pitchers in the late innings of games due to the few relievers of his day.

Records do not tell us how many of the home runs the great Bambino hit bounced over the low right field wall at Yankee Stadium. For the first 14 years of the Babe's career, ground-rule doubles counted as home runs.

There is no doubt that Hank Aaron was one of baseball's greatest home run hitters, and he accomplished his feat under the difficulty of modern-day relief pitching in full use. In comparing Williams and Aaron, the Thumper is ahead in home run percentage—6.8 to Aaron's 6.1—and in slugging percentage—.634 to Aaron's .555. Williams was the toughest slugger in baseball history to strike out. In his 7,706 at bats, he struck out only 709 times, which averages out to once in every 10.9 at bats. Aaron went down on strikes once in every 8.9 times, and the Babe was the easiest to whiff, as he went back to the dugout once in every 6.3 times at bat.

As far as total production is concerned, Williams ended up far below Ruth and Aaron, but that was due mainly to the 5 years of lost time Ted gave up serving his country in two wars. If his career home run percentage were applied for those five missing years, he would have hit close to 700 home runs.

A final tribute to Ted Williams can be made by recalling that he was the last Major Leaguer to bat over .400. In 1941 he batted .406 to gain this distinction, yet he was to lose the MVP award to Joe DiMaggio of the New York Yankees, who had had a fantastic season and hit in 56 consecutive games.

Only seven others have batted over .400 since 1901. Ty Cobb did it twice, batting .420 in 1911 before "slumping" to .410 in 1912. Nap Lajoie hit a marvelous .422 in 1901, and Shoeless Joe Jackson batted .408 *as a rookie* in 1911. (Ross Barnes was the first rookie, in 1876, the first year of baseball, to bat over .400, and Jackson was the last rookie to do it.) George Sisler hit over .400 twice. In 1920 he averaged .407, and he belted .420 in 1922. Harry Heilmann also accomplished the difficult feat by batting .403 in 1923.

In the National League Rogers Hornsby was one of two players to do it after 1900, and he didn't do it just once or twice. The player considered to be the best righthanded hitter in baseball hit over .400 three times. He hit .401 in 1922, .424 in 1924, and .403 in 1925.

The other player to reach that magic mark was Bill Terry of the Giants, who in 1930 was the last National Leaguer to obtain such heights.

All of the above-mentioned players are Hall of Famers except Joe Jackson, who was involved in the "Black Sox" scandal of the 1919 World Series.

Ted Williams won two MVP awards, the first in 1946 and the second in 1949. Oddly, he did not win the MVP in 1942 or 1947, the 2 years when he won the triple crown.

Tris Speaker's lifetime batting average was identical to Ted Williams's .344, and he was a genuine superstar as well. During his marvelous career of 22 years, Tris Speaker created an unbelievable total of 147 records! Of these records 24 are in the American League (12 unbroken), 14 are Major League marks (five unbroken), 12 are World Series records (three unbroken), 52 are Boston club records (seven unbroken), and 45 are Cleveland Indians club records (ten unbroken).

The reason why Tris Speaker has 45 Cleveland records is that Boston traded him in the prime of his career to Cleveland for Sad Sam Jones, Fred Thomas, and $55,000. Speaker responded to the trade by batting .386, .352, .318, .296, .388, .362, .378, .380, .344, .389, and .304 before he was sent to Washington and Philadelphia, where he ended his career in 1928.

On the other side of the trade, Sad Sam Jones was a sad replacement for Speaker. In six seasons he won only 64 games while losing 59. Thomas, a

CARL YASTRZEMSKI

RECORD PROFILE
CARL YASTRZEMSKI
CAREER BATTING RECORDS 1961–1983

Most Years	23	NEVER BROKEN
Most Games	3,308	NEVER BROKEN
Most Hits	3,419	NEVER BROKEN
Most Singles	2,262	NEVER BROKEN
Most Doubles	646	NEVER BROKEN
Most Extra Base Hits	1,157	NEVER BROKEN
Most Total Bases	5,539	NEVER BROKEN
Most Runs	1,816	NEVER BROKEN
Most RBIs	1,844	NEVER BROKEN
Most Strikeouts	1,393	NEVER BROKEN
Most At Bats	11,988	NEVER BROKEN

TED WILLIAMS

RECORD PROFILE
TED WILLIAMS
CAREER BATTING RECORDS 1939–1960

Most Years	19	20 years before broken
Most Games	2,292	17 years before broken
Most At Bats	7,706	14 years before broken
Most Hits	2,654	17 years before broken
Most Singles	1,537	17 years before broken
Most Doubles	525	19 years before broken
Most Home Runs	521	**NEVER BROKEN**
Highest Home Run Percentage	6.8	**NEVER BROKEN**
Most Grand Slams	17	**NEVER BROKEN**
Most Extra Base Hits	1,117	17 years before broken
Most Total Bases	4,884	17 years before broken
Most Runs	1,798	23 years before broken
Most RBIs	1,839	23 years before broken
Most Bases on Balls	2,018	**NEVER BROKEN**
Most Strikeouts	709	16 years before broken
Highest Batting Average	.344	**NEVER BROKEN**
Highest Slugging Percentage	.634	**NEVER BROKEN**
Most Pinch Hits	33	5 years before broken

third baseman, was sent to the minors in 1916 and 1917. He played 44 games in 1918 before being traded to the Athletics. His batting average with the Red Sox was only .225.

It was obvious that the Speaker trade was money-motivated, because it certainly wasn't due to a lack of production. Speaker had batted over .300 for seven consecutive seasons before money became more important to the club.

Tris Speaker was a league leader 24 times in various batting categories, and his specialty was hitting line-drive doubles. His 793 two baggers are the most in baseball history. He won the doubles title a record eight times!

But the "Gray Eagle," as he was called, was just as good with the leather as he was with the lumber. Amazingly, he was a fielding league leader 26 times!

Carl Yastrzemski will also go down as one of Boston's greatest players. His lifetime batting average of .285 is very deceiving, because his era (1961–83) was the most difficult in which to obtain a high average. Studies have been made comparing Yastrzemski's 1968 season, when he won the batting title by batting only .301, with other great players' seasons. It was the lowest average to win a batting title in history. The previous lows were .306 by Elmer Flick in 1905 and .309 by George Stirnweiss in 1945. When the degree of difficulty was measured, Yastrzemski's .301 average was cited as being equivalent to Bill Terry's .401 batting average that won the National League crown in 1929. Studies of course can be argued, but it is certain that there were fewer .300 hitters in the 1960s than ever before. The pitching had gotten better and better. In the past each club had one hurler who could throw in the 90s, but in the sixties several pitchers on each club had this ability. In addition to the exceptional power pitching, new pitches such as the slider (harder to hit than the curve) were driving the averages down. That, coupled with the specialization in relief pitching, made the .300 hitters fewer and farther between. There was a time when a good fastball and curve would produce a successful career, but with the addition of the slider and split-finger fastball the batters are finding it more and more difficult.

But even in those difficult times Carl Yastrzemski performed admirably, both at bat and in the field. He was the league leader 18 times in various batting categories. Three times he was the batting champion, slugging king, top doubles hitter, and runs scorer. He twice led in hits and bases on balls and once was the home run and RBI leader.

In the field he played the Green Monster like a master. He was a ten-time fielding leader (never once for most errors), and he even went through a full season without making a single error. Ken Harrelson had been the first Red Sox rightfielder to field 1.000, in 1968, and Yaz was the first and only leftfielder to work a perfecto, in 1977.

Yastrzemski's 23 years of service leaves him the senior statesman of the team. He established 19 club records, of which 13 remain unbroken. He should become the next Red Sox Hall of Famer. His greatest season came in 1967, when he won the MVP and triple crown.

CHAPTER VIII

CAREER PITCHING RECORDS

PITCHING QUIZ

1. This starting pitcher was elected to the Hall of Fame and has the most Red Sox wins. Name him.
2. Can you name the Red Sox starting pitcher who has the lowest ERA?
3. Do you know the Red Sox pitcher who has allowed the most bases on balls?
4. This Hall of Famer leads the club in strikeouts and shutouts. Do you know him?
5. Only one Red Sox pitcher has taken the mound for 12 years. Can you name him?

DID YOU KNOW that Cy Young established 15 Red Sox career pitching records and that 10 of them are still unbroken?

DID YOU KNOW that Bob Stanley has appeared in more games by far than any other pitcher in Boston history?

DID YOU KNOW that Dick Radatz was one of the most successful relief pitchers in Red Sox history? During his career he had 49 wins, 34 losses, and 100 saves.

Most Appearances

1903–06	Norwood Gibson	85
1902–07	Bill Dinneen	180
1901–08	Cy Young	*327
1948–55	Ellis Kinder	365
1977–88	**Bob Stanley**	**594**

Most Starts

1903–06	Norwood Gibson	72
1902–07	Bill Dinneen	175
1901–08	**Cy Young**	***298**

Most Complete Games

1903–06	Norwood Gibson	56
1902–07	Bill Dinneen	153
1901–08	**Cy Young**	***275**

Most Wins

1903–06	Norwood Gibson	34
1902–07	Bill Dinneen	87
1901–08	**Cy Young**	***193**

Most Losses

1903–06	Norwood Gibson	32
1902–07	Bill Dinneen	84
1901–08	**Cy Young**	**112**

Highest Winning Percentage

1903–06	Norwood Gibson	.515
1901–08	Cy Young	.632
1908–15	Joe Wood	.671
1945–50	**Boo Ferriss**	**.684**

Lowest ERA

1903–06	Norwood Gibson	2.93
1902–07	Bill Dinneen	2.80
1901–08	**Cy Young**	**2.01**

Most Innings

1903–06	Norwood Gibson	609
1902–07	Bill Dinneen	1,993
1901–08	**Cy Young**	***2,730**

Most Hits Allowed

1903–06	Norwood Gibson	525
1902–07	Bill Dinneen	1,330
1901–08	**Cy Young**	***2,347**

Most Bases on Balls

1903–06	Norwood Gibson	208
1902–07	Bill Dinneen	330
1901–08	George Winter	365
1908–15	Joe Wood	412
1947–56	**Mel Parnell**	**758**

Most Strikeouts

1903–06	Norwood Gibson	258
1902–07	Bill Dinneen	594
1901–08	**Cy Young**	**1,363**

Most Shutouts

1903–06	Norwood Gibson	3
1902–07	Bill Dinneen	16
1901–08	**Cy Young**	***39**

Most 20-Win Seasons

1901–08	**Cy Young**	6

Most Years

1903–06	Norwood Gibson	4
1902–07	Bill Dinneen	6
1901–08	Cy Young	8
1908–15	Joe Wood	8
1934–41	Lefty Grove	8
1941–49	Tex Hughson	9
1941–50	Joe Dobson	10
1947–56	Mel Parnell	10
1952–63	Ike Delock	11
1977–88	**Bob Stanley**	**12**

DID YOU KNOW that the two home runs Harry Hooper hit in the 1915 World Series were ruled "ground rule home runs"?

DID YOU KNOW that Ted Williams might have been a Yankee if his mother had accepted an offer from a Yankee scout?

DID YOU KNOW that Bobby Doerr is the only player to hit for the cycle twice for the Red Sox?

* American League Record
** Major League Record
*** Unbroken Major League Record

RELIEF PITCHING RECORDS

Most Appearances

1903–06	Norwood Gibson	13
1905–07	Joe Harris	13
1901–08	George Winter	*39
1908–12	Ed Cicotte	40
1909–13	Charley Hall	89
1934–37	Rube Walberg	90
1935–41	Jack Wilson	145
1941–46	Mike Ryba	156
1948–55	Ellis Kinder	276
1962–66	Dick Radatz	286
1977–88	**Bob Stanley**	**510**

Most Wins

1901–08	Cy Young	11
1909–13	Charley Hall	21
1935–41	Jack Wilson	26
1941–46	Mike Ryba	26
1948–55	Ellis Kinder	39
1962–66	Dick Radatz	49
1977–88	**Bob Stanley**	**79**

Most Losses

1901–08	George Winter	5
1909–13	Charley Hall	5
1912–14	Hugh Bedient	7
1915–18	Carl Mays	7
1920–21	Benn Karr	14
1935–41	Jack Wilson	17
1941–46	Mike Ryba	17
1948–55	Ellis Kinder	29
1962–66	Dick Radatz	34
1977–88	**Bob Stanley**	**55**

DID YOU KNOW that Boston General Manager Ed Borrow was responsible for making Babe Ruth an everyday player?

DID YOU KNOW that Babe Ruth would never have been sold to the Yankees if owner Harry Frazee's hit stage production had opened 2 months before instead of 2 months after the deal? Two months after the trade, Frazee netted $2 million on a play that solved all his financial problems.

Tom Meany on Babe Ruth: "He had the happy faculty of wearing the world as a loose garment."

Joe Dugan on Babe Ruth: "Born? The sonofabitch fell from a tree!"

Casey Stengel on Babe Ruth's pop-ups: "They'd be so high, everybody on the field thought they could get it. It looked like a union meetin'."

Babe Ruth to Connie Mack shortly before his death: "Hello, Mr. Mack, the termites have got me."

Tommy Holmes on Babe Ruth: "I stopped talking about him 20 years ago because I realized those who never saw him didn't believe me."

Larry Gardner describing a Babe Ruth home run: "The sound when he'd get a hold of one—it was just different, that's all."

Babe Ruth: "Bill Carrigan was the best manager I ever had."

Lefty Gomez: "Jimmy Foxx could hit me at midnight with the lights out."

Joe Cronin to an umpire about Bob Feller's fastball: "If I didn't see it, how did you see it?"

Ty Cobb: "Babe Ruth gave me more trouble than any other lefthanded pitcher."

Ted Williams: "In my heart I always felt I was the better hitter but Joe DiMaggio was the better player."

Dom DiMaggio: "Joe DiMaggio was the best righthanded hitter and Ted Williams the best lefthanded hitter."

Fred Lieb on Dom DiMaggio: "He looks like an assistant biology professor."

Most Saves

1901–08	Cy Young	9
1909–13	Charley Hall	16
1935–41	Jack Wilson	20
1948–55	Ellis Kinder	91
1962–66	Dick Radatz	100
1977–88	**Bob Stanley**	**128**

Most Wins Plus Saves

1901–08	Cy Young	20
1909–13	Charley Hall	37
1935–41	Jack Wilson	46
1948–55	Ellis Kinder	130
1962–66	Dick Radatz	149
1977–88	**Bob Stanley**	**207**

Highest Winning Percentage
(Minimum 25 Decisions)

1909–13	Charley Hall (21–5)	.807

Lowest ERA
(Minimum 25 Decisions)

1909–13	Charley Hall	2.93
1942–46	**Mace Brown**	**2.53**

Most Innings

1901–08	George Winter	39
1908–12	Ed Cicotte	48
1909–13	Charley Hall	171
1934–37	Rube Walberg	171
1935–41	Jack Wilson	377
1941–46	Mike Ryba	550
1948–55	Ellis Kinder	587
1977–88	**Bob Stanley**	**1,109**

Most Hits Allowed

1901–08	George Winter	32
1908–12	Ed Cicotte	36
1909–13	Charley Hall	146
1934–37	Rube Walberg	154
1935–41	Jack Wilson	320
1941–46	Mike Ryba	482
1948–55	Ellis Kinder	492
1977–88	**Bob Stanley**	**1,189**

Most Bases on Balls

1901–08	George Winter	10
1908–12	Ed Cicotte	13
1909–13	Charley Hall	53
1934–37	Rube Walberg	58

1935–41	Jack Wilson	189
1941–46	Mike Ryba	194
1948–55	Ellis Kinder	197
1962–66	Dick Radatz	202
1977–88	**Bob Stanley**	**316**

Most Strikeouts

1901–08	George Winter	15
1908–12	Ed Cicotte	19
1909–13	Charley Hall	66
1934–37	Rube Walberg	67
1935–41	Jack Wilson	215
1941–46	Mike Ryba	267
1948–55	Ellis Kinder	298
1962–66	**Dick Radatz**	**608**

Ken Harrelson: "Baseball is the only game when you're on offense the other team has the ball."

Connie Mack: "Joe Cronin was the best clutch hitter I ever saw, and that includes Ty Cobb."

Tris Speaker: "I could always hit, but not like Ted Williams. He was in a class by himself."

Sparky Anderson: "Tom Yawkey was the greatest gentleman I've ever met in baseball."

Dick Radatz: "We're not going to drink anymore—and we're not going to drink any less, either."

Joe DiMaggio: "Ted Williams was the best hitter I ever saw."

Ted Williams on Ted Williams: "All I ever wanted out of life was for people to say, 'There goes the greatest hitter who ever lived.' "

PITCHERS CAREER BATTING RECORDS		RECORD HOLDERS LIST		

PITCHERS CAREER BATTING RECORDS

Most At Bats

1901–08	Cy Young	1,050
1914–19	**Babe Ruth**	**†1,110**

Most Hits

1901–08	Cy Young	230
1914–19	**Babe Ruth**	**†342**

Most Home Runs

1901–08	Cy Young	6
1914–19	**Babe Ruth**	**†49**

Highest Batting Average

1904–07	Jesse Tannehill	.224
1909–11	Ed Karger	.233
1914–19	**Babe Ruth**	**†.308**

† These statistics include games in which Babe Ruth appeared as a player–pitcher.

RECORD HOLDERS LIST

1	Cy Young	16
2	Norwood Gibson	15
3	Bill Dinneen	13
4	Charley Hall	11
5	Bob Stanley	10
5	Ellis Kinder	10
7	Jack Wilson	9
8	Dick Radatz	7
8	Mike Ryba	7
10	Ed Cicotte	5
10	Rube Walberg	5
12	George Winter	4
13	Joe Wood	3
14	Joe Harris	2
14	Mel Parnell	2
16	Boo Ferriss	1
16	Lefty Grove	1
16	Tex Hughson	1
16	Carl Mays	1
16	Benn Karr	1
16	Hugh Bedient	1
16	Ike Delock	1
16	Job Dobson	1
16	Mace Brown	1

SUMMARY AND HIGHLIGHTS

Cy Young. Was he the greatest pitcher ever? If greatness is measured by most wins, then there is no doubt. Imagine winning 511 games—it is mind boggling, considering that today's standard of greatness is measured by 300 wins. Young pitched 7,356 innings—an average of over 340 innings per year. Very few pitchers now stay on the mound long enough to reach that figure—and Young did it year in, year out for 22 years. The burly right-hander started 815 games and completed 751.

Few realize that Cy Young was baseball's greatest control pitcher. He faced a total of 22,068 batters and issued only 1,217 bases on balls. That averages out to one walk every 18.1 batters. Of those 22,068 batters, only 7,092 of them got base hits, and 2,799 went down on strikes. When men are not on base, they can't score runs, and Young's outstanding ability to keep them off the bases resulted in a splendid career ERA of 2.63. Seventy-six games ended in shutouts, and 47 times Young was a league leader in various pitching departments. Perhaps what is even more amazing is that of the 22 years the great one pitched, he won 20 or more games 16 times! And 14 of those times were in a row!

One of the measurements of a great pitcher is how many more games he wins than loses. In this department the 6′ 2″ 210-pounder is number one again, as he shows 198 more wins than losses.

Baseball's winningest pitcher came to the Red Sox after having ten consecutive seasons in the National League in which he won 20 or more games. While with the Beantowners he had six more 20-or-more-win seasons. When it was thought that his career was near an end, he was traded to Cleveland, where he had a fine 19-win season before suffering two losing years before his retirement. In return for Young, the Red Sox received Charlie Check, Jack Ryan, and $12,500 cash. Neither Check nor Ryan were much help to Boston.

Our research has uncovered 149 records that Cy Young created (not including club records in the National League), including 42 American League marks (three unbroken), 14 National League records (two unbroken), 33 Major League marks (nine unbroken), 14 World Series records (all broken), and 47 Red Sox club records (15 unbroken).

Cy Young pitched three no-hitters during his marvelous career. The first was against Cincinnati in 1898, the second was against the Athletics in 1904 (perfect game), and the third was against the New York Yankees in 1908.

Cy Young entered the Hall of Fame in 1937, and his credentials will always remain undisputable. There will never be another pitcher like Cy Young.

Boo Ferriss, Tex Hughson, Mel Parnell, and Bob Stanley are the only big-name pitchers who have played their entire careers with the Red Sox. Of this group Mel Parnell was the most outstanding. Parnell only created one record, and it was a negative one at that. The smart lefthander issued more bases on balls than any other pitcher in Red Sox history. He is called smart because that is the way a lefthander had to pitch to survive in Fenway Park. It was imperative that he keep the ball away from right-handed hitters, and his bases on balls were augmented due to the fact that his 10 years of activity were one of the longest stints among pitchers on the team. Only Ike Delock and Bob Stanley have put on the Boston uniform more years, with Delock getting in 11 terms while Stanley is still active and in his 12th season.

Parnell did not get off to a good start, and his rookie season produced only two wins and three losses. But the cunning lefty then spun off winning seasons of 15, 25, 18, 18, 12, and 21 wins before nearing the end of his career.

Lefty Grove came to the Red Sox from the Athletics along with Rube Walberg and Max Bishop in exchange for Bob Kline, Rabbitt Warstler, and $125,000 in 1934. After Grove had a sensational 24–8 season for Connie Mack in 1933, the trade took place. Boston was taking a chance, due to the fact that lefthanders do not do well at Fenway Park as a result of the short left field wall. But Grove proved that lefthanders could do well. After an 8–8 season Grove, who was now in the twilight of his Hall of Fame career, had winning seasons of 20–12, 17–12, 17–9, 14–4, and 15–4. Certainly not

BOB STANLEY

RECORD PROFILE
BOB STANLEY
CAREER RELIEF PITCHING RECORDS

1977–88			
	Most Appearances	594	NEVER BROKEN
	Most Relief Appearances	510	NEVER BROKEN
	Most Wins	79	NEVER BROKEN
	Most Losses	55	NEVER BROKEN
	Most Saves	128	NEVER BROKEN
	Most Wins Plus Saves	207	NEVER BROKEN
	Most Innings	1,109	NEVER BROKEN
	Most Hits Allowed	1,189	NEVER BROKEN
	Most Bases on Balls	316	NEVER BROKEN
	Most Years	12	NEVER BROKEN

CY YOUNG

RECORD PROFILE
CY YOUNG
CAREER PITCHING RECORDS

1901–08			
	Most Appearances	327	47 years before broken
	Most Starts	298	**NEVER BROKEN**
	Most Complete Games	275	**NEVER BROKEN**
	Most Wins	193	**NEVER BROKEN**
	Most Losses	112	**NEVER BROKEN**
	Highest Winning Percentage	.632	7 years before broken
	Lowest ERA	2.01	**NEVER BROKEN**
	Most Innings	2,730	**NEVER BROKEN**
	Most Hits Allowed	2,347	**NEVER BROKEN**
	Most Strikeouts	1,363	**NEVER BROKEN**
	Most Shutouts	39	**NEVER BROKEN**
	Most 20-Win Seasons	6	**NEVER BROKEN**
	Most Years	8	41 years before broken
	Most Relief Wins	11	5 years before broken
	Most Saves	9	5 years before broken
	Most Wins Plus Saves	20	14 years before broken

bad for a lefty at Fenway—and an old man of 17 seasons on the mound. He was 41 years old when he finally hung up his spikes.

What was most impressive about Grove's performance was that in four of his last five seasons he led the league in the ERA department! But leading the league in this category was not new to the 6′ 3″ 190-pounder. In all he won nine ERA titles! Add to that four most wins crowns (eight 20-or-more-win seasons), five highest winning percentage titles (.680, second best), seven consecutive years of winning the strikeout title, and three years of leading the league in shutouts. Grove also had 3 consecutive years of completing more games than any other American League pitcher, appeared in the most games in 1930, started the most games in 1929, and even had the most saves in 1930. In all Lefty Grove led the league 35 times!

During Grove's spectacular 17-year career, he amassed 33 records, of which 12 remain unbroken. These include 12 American League (four unbroken), 11 Major League (four unbroken), three All-Star (three unbroken), two World Series (one unbroken), four Athletic club records (two unbroken), and one Red Sox club record (unbroken). He became a Hall of Famer in 1947.

Ellis Kinder was traded to Boston from the old St. Louis Browns along with Billy Hitchcock for Sam Dente, Clem Dreisewerd, Bill Sommers, and $65,000. Kinder paid his debt to the Red Sox by becoming one of their most successful relief pitchers. In 8 years the 215-pound righthander won 86, lost 52, and saved 91. Kinder served his first three seasons as a starter and had his best year in 1949, when he won 23 and lost only six times. He switched to the bullpen in 1951 and promptly led the league in appearances with 63, in wins with ten, and in saves with 14! In that marvelous 1951 season Kinder suffered only one loss to go along with his ten wins. The big righty still had some good years in him and in 1953 had another super season in relief. He improved his own marks in appearances to 69 and saves to 27 and tossed in ten more wins. He was traded to the Cardinals in 1956 for the waiver price, and his career ended with the White Sox in 1957.

CHAPTER IX

CAREER FIELDING RECORDS

FIELDING QUIZ

1. Do you know the Red Sox first baseman who has the longest career?
2. Can you name the Red Sox second baseman who has the highest fielding percentage?
3. Can you name the Red Sox third baseman who owns five unbroken records?
4. Who was the first Red Sox third baseman to record 1,000 or more assists?
5. This fine Red Sox shortstop has turned the most double plays and also has the highest fielding percentage. Name him.

DID YOU KNOW that Ted Williams has more putouts and total chances than any other leftfielder in Red Sox history?

DID YOU KNOW that Duffy Lewis played only 8 years to Ted Williams's 19 years in left field, yet has more assists, errors, and double plays?

DID YOU KNOW that Dwight Evans has played the most games and has the most putouts and total chances of any rightfielder in Red Sox history?

FIRST BASE

Most Years

1902–05	Candy LaChance	*4
1908–13	Jake Stahl	5
1914–18	Dick Hobitzell	5
1924–30	Phil Todt	7
1936–42	Jimmy Foxx	7
1966–79	George Scott	9
1968–83	**Carl Yastrzemski**	†15

Most Games

1902–05	Candy LaChance	*448
1914–18	Dick Hobitzell	448
1918–21	Stuffy McInnis	512
1924–30	Phil Todt	852
1966–79	**George Scott**	**992**

Most Putouts

1902–05	Candy LaChance	*4,706
1918–21	Stuffy McInnis	5,437
1924–30	**Phil Todt**	**8,518**

Most Assists

1902–05	Candy LaChance	*162
1908–13	Jake Stahl	204
1914–18	Dick Hobitzell	212
1918–21	Stuffy McInnis	346
1924–30	**Phil Todt**	**599**

Most Errors

1902–05	Candy LaChance	*66
1908–13	Jake Stahl	73
1924–30	Phil Todt	75
1966–79	**George Scott**	**95**

Most Double Plays

1902–05	Candy LaChance	*213
1918–21	Stuffy McInnis	339
1924–30	Phil Todt	669
1936–42	Jimmy Foxx	679
1966–79	**George Scott**	**724**

Most Chances Per Game

1902–05	Candy LaChance	*11.3
1918–21	**Stuffy McInnis**	**11.4**

Most Total Chances

1902–05	Candy LaChance	*4,934
1918–21	Stuffy McInnis	5,807
1924–30	**Phil Todt**	**9,192**

Highest Fielding Percentage

1902–05	Candy LaChance	*.986
1914–18	Dick Hobitzell	.986
1918–21	**Stuffy McInnis**	**.995**
1968–83	**Carl Yastrzemski**	**.995**

SECOND BASE

Most Years

1901–07	Hobe Ferris	7
1937–51	**Bobby Doerr**	**14**

Most Games

1901–07	Hobe Ferris	983
1937–51	**Bobby Doerr**	**1,852**

Most Putouts

1901–07	Hobe Ferris	2,410
1937–51	**Bobby Doerr**	**4,834**

Most Assists

1901–07	Hobe Ferris	3,063
1937–51	**Bobby Doerr**	**5,586**

Most Errors

1901–07	Hobe Ferris	261

Most Double Plays

1901–07	Hobe Ferris	341
1926–30	Bill Regan	387
1937–51	**Bobby Doerr**	**1,487**

Most Chances Per Game

1901–07	Hobe Ferris	5.8
1926–30	**Bill Regan**	**5.9**
1937–51	**Bobby Doerr**	**5.9**

Most Total Chances

1901–07	Hobe Ferris	5,734
1937–51	**Bobby Doerr**	**10,628**

---

* American League Record
** Major League Record
*** Unbroken Major League Record

† In most years Yaz was played sparingly at first.

Highest Fielding Percentage

1901–07	Hobe Ferris	.954
1926–30	Bill Regan	.962
1937–51	Bobby Doerr	**.980
1961–65	Chuck Schilling	.982

SHORTSTOP

Most Years

1901–07	Freddy Parent	*7
1914–21	Everett Scott	8
1908–16	Heinie Wagner	8
1935–42	Joe Cronin	8
1963–76	Rico Petrocelli	8

Most Games

1901–07	Freddy Parent	*909
1914–21	Everett Scott	1,093

Most Putouts

1901–07	Freddy Parent	*1,971
1914–21	Everett Scott	2,310

Most Assists

1901–07	Freddy Parent	*3,015
1914–21	Everett Scott	3,394

Most Errors

1901–07	Freddy Parent	*388

Most Double Plays

1901–07	Freddy Parent	*308
1914–21	Everett Scott	440
1935–42	Joe Cronin	565
1974–80	Rick Burleson	657

Most Chances Per Game

1901–07	Freddy Parent	*5.7
1908–16	Heinie Wagner	6.0

Ty Cobb: "I never let Tris Speaker know how much I admired him until we became teammates in 1928."

Harry Hooper: "Babe Ruth could eat more than anyone and hit a ball farther than anyone."

Most Total Chances

1901–07	Freddy Parent	*5,374
1914–21	Everett Scott	5,904

Highest Fielding Percentage

1901–07	Freddy Parent	.928
1908–16	Heinie Wagner	.931
1914–21	Everett Scott	**.965
1942–52	Johnny Pesky	.965
1963–76	Rico Petrocelli	.968
1974–80	Rick Burleson	.970

THIRD BASE

Most Years

1901–07	Jimmy Collins	*7
1908–17	Larry Gardner	9
1955–65	Frank Malzone	11

Most Games

1901–07	Jimmy Collins	735
1908–17	Larry Gardner	928
1955–65	Frank Malzone	1,335

Most Putouts

1901–07	Jimmy Collins	925
1908–17	Larry Gardner	1,003
1955–65	Frank Malzone	1,244

Most Assists

1901–07	Jimmy Collins	1,503
1908–17	Larry Gardner	1,809
1955–65	Frank Malzone	2,752

Most Errors

1901–07	Jimmy Collins	*174
1908–17	Larry Gardner	175
1938–44	Jim Tabor	182
1955–65	Frank Malzone	182

Most Double Plays

1901–07	Jimmy Collins	*86
1908–17	Larry Gardner	108
1938–44	Jim Tabor	151
1955–65	Frank Malzone	281

Most Chances Per Game

1901–07	Jimmy Collins	3.6

Most Total Chances

1901–07	Jimmy Collins	2,602
1908–17	Larry Gardner	2,987
1955–65	**Frank Malzone**	**4,178**

Highest Fielding Percentage

1901–07	Jimmy Collins	.927
1908–17	Larry Gardner	.942
1955–65	Frank Malzone	.957
1966–76	**Rico Petrocelli**	**.969**

CATCHING

Most Years

1901–08	Lou Criger	*8
1906–16	Bill Carrigan	10
1969–80	**Carlton Fisk**	**11**

Most Games

1901–08	Lou Criger	*613
1906–16	Bill Carrigan	648
1969–80	**Carlton Fisk**	**990**

Most Putouts

1901–08	Lou Criger	2,830
1951–59	Sammy White	4,443
1969–80	**Carlton Fisk**	**5,037**

Most Assists

1901–08	Lou Criger	*870

Most Errors

1901–08	Lou Criger	95
1969–80	**Carlton Fisk**	**96**

Most Double Plays

1901–08	Lou Criger	*62
1951–59	**Sammy White**	**77**

Most Chances Per Game

1901–08	**Lou Criger**	**6.2**
1906–16	**Bill Carrigan**	**6.2**

Most Total Chances

1901–08	Lou Criger	3,795
1951–59	Sammy White	4,990
1969–80	**Carlton Fisk**	**5,607**

Highest Fielding Percentage

1901–08	Lou Criger	*.974
1947–50	Birdie Tebbetts	.980
1951–59	**Sammy White**	**.984**

LEFT FIELD

Most Years

1902–04	Pat Dougherty	3
1910–17	Duffy Lewis	8
1940–60	**Ted Williams**	**18**

Most Games

1902–04	Pat Dougherty	290
1910–17	Duffy Lewis	*1,165
1940–60	**Ted Williams**	**2,002**

Most Putouts

1902–04	Pat Dougherty	524
1910–17	Duffy Lewis	*2,174
1940–60	**Ted Williams**	**3,837**

Most Assists

1902–04	Pat Dougherty	28
1910–17	**Duffy Lewis**	***180**

Most Errors

1902–04	Pat Dougherty	42
1910–17	**Duffy Lewis**	**110**

Most Double Plays

1902–04	Pat Dougherty	7
1910–17	**Duffy Lewis**	***35**

Most Chances Per Game

1902–04	Pat Dougherty	2.0
1910–17	Duffy Lewis	*2.1
1975–87	**Jim Rice**	**2.1**

Most Total Chances

1902–04	Pat Dougherty	594
1910–17	Duffy Lewis	*2,464
1940–60	**Ted Williams**	**4,060**

Highest Fielding Percentage

1902–04	Pat Dougherty	.925
1910–17	Duffy Lewis	.954
1940–60	Ted Williams	.974
1975–87	**Jim Rice**	**.986**

CENTER FIELD		RIGHT FIELD	

Most Years

1901–06	Chick Stahl	*6
1907–15	Tris Speaker	9
1941–53	**Dom DiMaggio**	**10**

Most Years

1901–07	Buck Freeman	*7
1909–19	Harry Hooper	11
1972–88	**Dwight Evans**	**17**

Most Games

1901–06	Chick Stahl	776
1907–15	Tris Speaker	1,053
1941–53	**Dom DiMaggio**	**1,279**

Most Games

1901–07	Buck Freeman	*556
1909–19	Harry Hooper	*1,517
1972–88	**Dwight Evans**	**2,001**

Most Putouts

1901–06	Chick Stahl	*1,542
1907–15	Tris Speaker	2,500
1941–53	**Dom DiMaggio**	**3,620**

Most Putouts

1901–07	Buck Freeman	*865
1909–19	Harry Hooper	*2,494
1972–88	**Dwight Evans**	**4,007**

Most Assists

| 1901–06 | Chick Stahl | 79 |
| **1907–15** | **Tris Speaker** | **196** |

Most Assists

| 1901–07 | Buck Freeman | *55 |
| **1909–19** | **Harry Hooper** | ***238** |

Most Errors

| 1901–06 | Chick Stahl | *64 |
| **1907–15** | **Tris Speaker** | **109** |

Most Errors

| 1901–07 | Buck Freeman | 40 |
| **1909–19** | **Harry Hooper** | ***101** |

Most Double Plays

| 1901–06 | Chick Stahl | 20 |
| **1907–15** | **Tris Speaker** | **60** |

Most Double Plays

| 1901–07 | Buck Freeman | 9 |
| **1909–19** | **Harry Hooper** | ***54** |

Most Chances Per Game

1901–06	Chick Stahl	*2.1
1907–15	Tris Speaker	2.7
1941–53	**Dom DiMaggio**	**3.0**

Most Chances Per Game

1901–07	Buck Freeman	*1.6
1909–19	Harry Hooper	*1.9
1955–61	Jackie Jensen	2.0
1972–88	**Dwight Evans**	**2.1**

Most Total Chances

1901–06	Chick Stahl	*1,685
1907–15	Tris Speaker	2,805
1941–53	**Dom DiMaggio**	**3,834**

Most Total Chances

1901–07	Buck Freeman	*967
1909–19	Harry Hooper	*2,833
1972–88	**Dwight Evans**	**4,273**

Highest Fielding Percentage

1901–06	Chick Stahl	*.962
1924–28	Ira Flagstead	.978
1950–58	**Jimmy Piersall**	****.990**

Highest Fielding Percentage

1901–07	Buck Freeman	*.948
1909–19	Harry Hooper	.963
1955–61	Jackie Jensen	.974
1965–70	Tony Conigliaro	.980
1972–88	**Dwight Evans**	**.988**

Joe DiMaggio to brother Dom: "I bet you felt like cutting my throat after I hit that home run against you." Dom: "Don't tell my manager, but I felt like applauding you too."

Billy Conigliaro: "They're going to retire my uniform . . . with me in it."

RECORD HOLDERS LIST

1	Candy LaChance	9
1	Freddy Parent	9
1	Hobe Ferris	9
1	Jimmy Collins	9
1	Lou Criger	9
1	Pat Dougherty	9
1	Chick Stahl	9
1	Buck Freeman	9
1	Duffy Lewis	9
1	Harry Hooper	9
11	Tris Speaker	8
11	Bobby Doerr	8
11	Larry Gardner	8
11	Frank Malzone	8
15	Stuffy McInnis	7
15	Phil Todt	7
15	Everett Scott	7
18	Dwight Evans	6
19	Carlton Fisk	5
19	Dom DiMaggio	5
19	Ted Williams	5
22	Dick Hobitzell	4
22	George Scott	4
22	Sammy White	4
25	Jake Stahl	3
25	Bill Regan	3
27	Rick Burleson	2
27	Heinie Wagner	2
27	Jim Tabor	2
27	Jimmy Foxx	2
27	Jackie Jensen	2
27	Carl Yastrzemski	2
27	Joe Cronin	2
27	Bill Carrigan	2
27	Rico Petrocelli	2
27	Jim Rice	2
37	Chuck Schilling	1
37	Johnny Pesky	1
37	Birdie Tebbetts	1
37	Ira Flagstead	1
37	Jimmy Piersall	1
37	Tony Conigliaro	1

SUMMARY AND HIGHLIGHTS

Carl Yastrzemski's 15 years at first base is deceiving because he was better known and played more games in left field. Yaz played only 765 games at first, most of them at the end of his career, but earlier on he was regularly called upon to play 10 to 15 games there during the season. George Scott, Jimmy Foxx, and Phil Todt did some excellent work around the bag, but Boston's best-fielding first baseman was Stuffy McInnis. The smooth-fielding righthanded first baseman was only with the Red Sox for four full seasons, and his .995 fielding average has only been matched 50 and more years later by Carl Yastrzemski.

At second base, Hall of Famer Bobby Doerr led the league in fielding more times than any other Red Sox second baseman. In fact, his 24 league-leading stats are more than any other player on the entire team. Even more impressive is the fact that Doerr never led the league in errors. He was a master at turning the double play and was a league leader in that category five times. Four times he was the most active second baseman in putouts, total chances per game, and total chances. He also led the league in fielding percentage four times and was the assist leader three times. Doerr's 14 years at second is far more than any other player, and as a result he holds unbroken records for games, putouts, assists, double plays, chances per game, and total chances. Even though he played twice as many years as any other second baseman, the sure-handed second sacker did not make the most errors! Chuck Schilling shows a two-point edge in fielding percentage, but Schilling played only 5 years, compared to Doerr's 14. Schilling also had the advantage of using a more modern glove.

The Red Sox have had four players at shortstop for 8-year careers. The best of them was Everett Scott. Scott starred from 1914 to 1921 and led the league 13 times in various fielding categories. Never did he embarrass himself by being the leader in errors. On the contrary, Scott led the league in fielding percentage 6 consecutive years, from 1916 to 1921. He also recorded the most putouts and double plays twice and was a one-time champion in assists, total chances per game, and total chances. No Red Sox

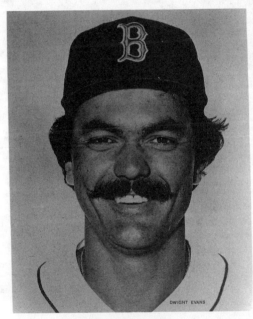

DWIGHT EVANS

RECORD PROFILE
DWIGHT EVANS
CAREER FIELDING RECORDS RIGHT FIELD
1972–1988

Most Years	17	NEVER BROKEN
Most Games	1,917	NEVER BROKEN
Most Putouts	3,926	NEVER BROKEN
Most Chances Per Game	2.2	NEVER BROKEN
Most Total Chances	4,117	NEVER BROKEN
Highest Fielding Percentage	.988	NEVER BROKEN

BOBBY DOERR

RECORD PROFILE
BOBBY DOERR
CAREER FIELDING RECORDS SECOND BASE
1937–51

Most Years	14	NEVER BROKEN
Most Games	1,852	NEVER BROKEN
Most Putouts	4,834	NEVER BROKEN
Most Assists	5,586	NEVER BROKEN
Most Double Plays	1,487	NEVER BROKEN
Most Chances Per Game	5.9	NEVER BROKEN
Most Total Chances	10,628	NEVER BROKEN
Highest Fielding Percentage	.980	14 years before broken

shortstop has played as many games or registered more putouts, assists, or total chances. And this record has stood since 1921!

At third base, top honors go to Frank Malzone, who was a league leader 20 times at that position. Malzone was a brick wall at the hot corner from 1955 to 1965. Five times he participated in more double plays than any other third baseman. Three times he was the most active in assists, total chances per game, and total chances, and once he led the league in putouts and fielding average. The only negative in Malzone's career is that he also led the league in errors four times.

Carlton Fisk is the dean of catchers. After 11 years of work behind the plate, this fine catcher tallied nine league-leading marks.

Boston's most outstanding defensive catcher was Sammy White, who put on the tools of ignorance from 1951 to 1959. During that time White led the league 11 times and only once in errors. Four times he was the leader in assists, which points out two very important strong points as a catcher. It means that he was quick enough to field bunts and had a strong and accurate arm to throw runners going to second or third. In addition to these fine qualities, White's .984 career fielding percentage is the best in Red Sox history.

In left field, the choice for the top man is exceptionally easy. No one played the Green Monster better than Carl Yastrzemski. His specialty was catching balls off the wall and throwing runners out at second base. This is clearly seen by his seven seasons of leading the league in assists. In all Yaz was a league leader ten times and only once did he make the most errors. But he more than made up for that when he led the league in fielding average in 1977 by posting a perfect season.

The Red Sox have had three exceptional centerfielders in Tris Speaker, Dom DiMaggio, and Jimmy Piersall. Speaker was the first superstar in that position, and his 21 times of leading the league in fielding is a record for Boston outfielders. Speaker had outstanding speed as well as a fine throwing arm. Five times he led in putouts and total chances per game, three times he led in assists and total chances, four times he led in double plays, and only once did he make the most errors.

Dom DiMaggio, whom brother Joe says was the best centerfielder he ever saw, racked up 14 league-leading titles in the field. His exceptional speed enabled him to reach more balls than most centerfielders, and as a result he was a two-time leader in putouts, assists, errors, and double plays. Four times he set most chances per game highs.

Jimmy Piersall could run down a fly ball with the best of them, and his four full seasons in the main field produced a club-leading .990 fielding percentage. Seven times he led the league, doing it twice in putouts, total chances per game, and total chances. Once he had the highest fielding percentage, and he never made the most errors.

Boston's most active rightfielders were Harry Hooper, who starred from 1909 to 1919, and Dwight Evans, who began his career in 1972 and is still playing. It is difficult to pick a number-one man in this position because each led the league only three times. Hooper led once in assists, double plays, and errors, while Evans, using his powerful throwing arm, was twice a leader in double plays (before runners stopped trying to take the extra base on him) and once led the league in fielding percentage.

CHAPTER X

COMPOSITE RECORD HOLDERS LISTS

Here is a summing up of the records of all players in all categories.

It is important to note that the players with the most records may not be the team's greatest players. The following list, therefore, is *not* a ranking of players in the order of their greatness.

The reason for this is that the records must have a starting point, and those players who are at the starting points will post many records because none stood before them. What is more important than the quantity of records is the quality and longevity of records.

Records are not the only means for measuring a player's greatness, but it cannot be denied that great players will tend to create records that will stand the test of time.

The following chapter will present two separate lists. One is for everyday players, while the other is for pitchers only.

EVERYDAY PLAYERS

1	Freddy Parent	61
2	Ted Williams	*55
3	Tris Speaker	*52
3	Harry Hooper	*52
5	Buck Freeman	49
5	Pat Dougherty	49
7	Duffy Lewis	43
7	Hobe Ferris	43
9	Chick Stahl	38
10	Candy LaChance	35
11	Lou Criger	32
12	Bobby Doerr	*29
13	Jimmy Collins	*27
14	Everett Scott	24
15	Harry Gleason	23
17	Stuffy McInnis	22
18	Jimmy Foxx	*20
19	Carl Yastrzemski	19
20	Heinie Wagner	16
21	Johnny Pesky	15
21	Frank Malzone	15
21	Ike Boone	15
24	Babe Ruth	*14
24	Phil Todt	14
24	Tommy Oliver	14
26	Moose Grimshaw	13
26	Denny Sullivan	13
26	Dom DiMaggio	13
29	Tommy Dowd	12
30	Harry Lord	10
31	George Scott	9
31	Sammy White	9
31	Chuck Schilling	9
31	Jim Tabor	9
35	Joe Cronin	*8
35	Charlie Hemphill	8
35	Carlton Fisk	8
35	Red Morgan	8
35	Bill Carrigan	8
35	Charlie Armbruster	8
41	Doug Taitt	7
41	John Hoey	7
41	Dwight Evans	7
41	Bill Regan	7
41	Reggie Smith	7
46	Jim Rice	6
46	Babe Dahlgren	6

* Hall of Famer.

46	Bill Wambsganss	6
46	Amby McConnell	6
46	Ira Flagstead	6
46	Mike Menosky	6
46	Fred Lynn	6
52	Jake Stahl	5
52	Roy Partee	5
52	Rick Burleson	5
52	Rick Ferrell	*5
52	Mike Ryan	5
52	Jimmy Piersall	5
52	Rico Petrocelli	5
59	Tex Vache	4
59	Walt Dropo	4
59	Vern Stephens	4
59	John Pagliaroni	4
59	Dick Hoblitzell	4
59	Jack Rothrock	4
59	Jackie Jensen	4
59	Harry Niles	4
59	Chick Shorten	4
59	Sam Mele	4
69	Dalton Jones	3
69	Jack Thoney	3
69	Wade Boggs	3
69	Bob Tillman	3
69	Roy Johnson	3
69	Ossie Vitt	3
69	Russ Nixon	3
69	Oscar Melillo	3
77	Urbane Pickering	2
77	Sam Horn	2
77	Roy Carlyle	2
77	Doc Cramer	2
77	Earl Webb	2
77	Duke Farrell	2
77	Dick Stuart	2
77	Ossee Schreckengost	2
77	Del Pratt	2
77	Jack Barry	2
77	Steve Yerkes	2
77	Gavvy Cravath	2
77	Norm Zauchin	2
77	Marv Olson	2
77	Bob Unglaub	2
77	Bill Conroy	2
77	Pete Fox	2
77	Buddy Myer	2
77	Amos Strunk	2
77	Bunk Congalton	2

77	Rick Miller	2
77	Charlie Berry	2
77	Grady Hatton	2
77	Gene De Sautels	2
77	Lee Thomas	2
77	Ben Chapman	2
77	Ken Harrelson	2
77	Tony Lupien	2
77	Billy Goodman	2
77	Milt Bolling	2
77	Billy Conigliaro	2
77	Ellis Burks	2
109	Jesse Burkett	*1
109	Frank Pytlak	1
109	Rich Gedman	1
109	Jimmy Barrett	1
109	Alex Gaston	1
109	Butch Hobson	1
109	Roxy Walters	1
109	Topper Rigney	1
109	Kip Selbach	1
109	Jack O'Brien	1
109	Lenny Green	1
109	Ken Williams	1
109	Vic Wertz	1
109	Rudy York	1
109	Eddie Lake	1
109	Fred Haney	1
109	Hick Cady	1
109	Muddy Ruel	1
109	Birdie Tebbetts	1
109	Tony Conigliaro	1
109	Charley Metkovich	1
109	Doc Gessler	1
109	Don Baylor	1
109	Wally Schang	1
109	Hal Janvrin	1
109	Babe Dahlgren	1
109	Dick Gernert	1
109	Red Nonnenkamp	1
109	Stan Spence	1
109	Tommy Umphlett	1
109	Don Buddin	1
109	Bing Miller	1
109	Gene Stephens	1

PITCHERS

1	Cy Young	*47
2	Dick Radatz	28
3	Ellis Kinder	25
4	Charley Hall	23
5	Norwood Gibson	22
6	Bill Dinneen	20
7	George Winter	19
8	Joe Wood	15
8	Carl Mays	15
10	Joe Harris	13
10	Bob Stanley	13
12	Ed Cicotte	10
12	Jack Wilson	10
14	Hugh Bedient	9
14	Tex Pruiett	9
16	Tony Welzer	8
16	Mike Ryba	8
18	Frank Barrett	6
18	Murray Wall	6
20	Buck O'Brien	5
20	Wilcy Moore	5
20	Rube Walberg	5
23	Mace Brown	4
23	Benn Karr	4
23	Frank Arellanes	4
23	Boo Ferriss	4
23	Ike Delock	4
23	Tom Hurd	4
29	Ralph Glaze	3
29	Mel Parnell	3
29	Mike Forniles	3
29	Joe Heving	3
29	Fred Mitchell	3
34	Howard Ehmke	2
34	Bill Campbell	2
34	Johnny Welch	2
34	Jack Lamabe	2
38	Ed Morris	1
38	Babe Ruth	*1
38	Slim Harriss	1
38	Red Ruffing	*1
38	Jesse Tannehill	1
38	Jim Willoughby	1
38	Joe Dobson	1
38	Lefty Grove	*1
38	Buster Ross	1
38	Elmer Steele	1
38	Don Schwall	1

38	Ted Wingfield	1	38	Calvin Schiraldi	1
38	Mike Nagy	1	38	Ernie Shore	1
38	Wes Ferrell	1	38	Tex Hughson	1
38	Earl Wilson	1	38	Roger Clemens	1

CHAPTER XI

MANAGERS SEASON AND CAREER RECORDS

MANAGERS QUIZ

1. In 1903 Boston won its first pennant. Can you name the manager, who was also the team's third baseman?
2. Only two Boston managers have won two consecutive pennants. Can you name them?
3. In 1912 this Red Sox manager became the first to win more than 100 games in a season. Do you know him?
4. Can you name the Red Sox manager who has the highest career winning percentage?
5. Which Red Sox manager has had the longest career?

DID YOU KNOW that the Red Sox won the pennant in 1904, but there was no World Series because the leagues were at war with each other?

DID YOU KNOW that Joe Cronin is the only Boston manager who has more than 1,000 wins?

DID YOU KNOW that Jimmy Collins was the first Boston manager and that he accounted for 24 records?

SEASON RECORDS

Most Wins
1901	Jimmy Collins	79
1903	Jimmy Collins	*91
1904	Jimmy Collins	*95
1912	Jake Stahl	*105

Most Losses
1901	Jimmy Collins	57
1902	Jimmy Collins	60
1905	Jimmy Collins	74
1906	Jimmy Collins	92
1922	Hugh Duffy	93
1925	Lee Fohl	105
1926	Lee Fohl	107

Highest Winning Percentage
1901	Jimmy Collins	.581
1903	Jimmy Collins	*.659
1912	Jake Stahl	*.691

Highest Finish
1901	Jimmy Collins	2nd
1903	Jimmy Collins	1st
1904	Jimmy Collins	1st
1912	Jake Stahl	1st
1915	Bill Carrigan	1st
1916	Bill Carrigan	1st
1918	Ed Barrow	1st
1946	Joe Cronin	1st
1967	Dick Williams	1st
1975	Darrell Johnson	1st
1986	John McNamara	1st
1988	Joe Morgan	1st

Most Games Won Pennant By
1903	Jimmy Collins	*14½

CAREER RECORDS

Most Years
1901–06	Jimmy Collins	*6
1913–29	Bill Carrigan	7
1935–47	Joe Cronin	13

Most Games
1901–06	Jimmy Collins	*853
1913–29	Bill Carrigan	989
1935–47	Joe Cronin	1,987

Most Wins
1901–06	Jimmy Collins	*464
1913–29	Bill Carrigan	489
1935–47	Joe Cronin	1,071

Most Losses
1901–06	Jimmy Collins	*389
1913–29	Bill Carrigan	500
1935–47	Joe Cronin	916

Highest Winning Percentage
1901–06	Jimmy Collins	*.544
1976–80	Don Zimmer	.571

Most Pennants Won
1901–06	Jimmy Collins	*2
1913–29	Bill Carrigan	2

Most World Series Won
1901–06	Jimmy Collins	*1
1905–13	Jake Stahl	*1
1913–29	Bill Carrigan	2

Most World Series Games
1901–06	Jimmy Collins	*8
1905–13	Jake Stahl	*8
1913–29	Bill Carrigan	10

Most World Series Games Won
1901–06	Jimmy Collins	*5
1913–29	Bill Carrigan	8

Most World Series Games Lost
1901–06	Jimmy Collins	**3
1912–13	Jake Stahl	*3
1935–47	Joe Cronin	4
1967–69	Dick Williams	4
1974–76	Darrell Johnson	4
1986–87	John McNamara	4

---

* American League Record
** Major League Record
*** Unbroken Major League Record

DID YOU KNOW that Joe Cronin was only 26 years old when he managed the Washington Senators to a pennant?

Highest World Series Winning Percentage

1901–06 Jimmy Collins	.625
1913–29 Bill Carrigan	.800

Most Divisional Titles

1974–76 Darrell Johnson	1
1986–87 John McNamara	1
1988 Joe Morgan	1

Most Playoff Games

1974–76 Darrell Johnson	3
1986–87 John McNamara	7

Most Playoff Games Won

1974–76 Darrell Johnson	3
1986–87 John McNamara	4

Most Playoff Games Lost

1986–87 John McNamara	3
1988 Joe Morgan	4

RECORD HOLDERS LIST

1	Jimmy Collins	24
2	Bill Carrigan	11
3	John McNamara	6
3	Jake Stahl	6
5	Joe Cronin	5
6	Darrell Johnson	4
7	Joe Morgan	3
8	Lee Fohl	2
8	Dick Williams	2
10	Don Zimmer	1
10	Ed Barrow	1
10	Hugh Duffy	1

SUMMARY AND HIGHLIGHTS

Jimmy Collins was the first Red Sox manager, and he did well in bringing Boston its first two pennants, in 1903 and 1904. Collins was a successful World Series manager in his first attempt in 1903, which was the first World Series (played in modern times) between the two leagues. Collins was denied a second chance at winning a World Series in 1904 because of executive feuding. The National League, angry at Ban Johnson (the American League's president) for stealing National League talent, refused to accept the American League's status as a major league. But the leagues came to their senses in 1905 and the World Series tradition continued—but the Red Sox would have to wait 7 years before they would play in one again.

Jimmy Collins held two jobs at the same time while with the Red Sox. He was both their regular third baseman and their team manager. Player-managers are rare today, but prior to 1900 there were many of them. Collins did his job well, winning 464 games from 1901 to 1906 while bringing the team in second in 1901 before winning in 1903 and 1904. His 1903 victory was by 14½ games, the largest margin of victory in Boston history.

Collins played well enough to be voted into the Hall of Fame in 1945. He possessed unusual power for a little man of 5' 7½" and 160 pounds. Even though he played in the dead-ball era, the hustler from Buffalo, New York, banged 64 homers, 116 triples, and 352 doubles. His greatest moment came in 1898, when he led the National League in home runs with 15 and in home run percentage at 2.5. Five times he batted over .300, with a career high of .346 in 1897.

During his exciting 14-year career, Collins established a fabulous total of 99 records. He set two in the National League and eight in the American

JOE CRONIN

RECORD PROFILE
JOE CRONIN
MANAGERS CAREER RECORDS
1935–47

Most Years	13	NEVER BROKEN
Most Games	1,987	NEVER BROKEN
Most Wins	1,071	NEVER BROKEN
Most Losses	916	NEVER BROKEN
Most World Series Games Lost	4	Tied

League; four were Major League marks, 11 were Boston Braves club records, 29 were Boston Red Sox club records, 21 were World Series marks, and 24 were managerial records.

Bill Carrigan was the second outstanding manager. His nickname was "Rough," and he was a catcher by trade. Carrigan was also a player-manager, from 1913 to 1916. He, like Jimmy Collins, played very well, but he was a better manager than a player. He caught and led the team to back-to-back pennants and World Series wins in 1915 and 1916, even though he batted only .200 and .270. But at this time in his career he only served to rest his other catchers.

As a player he worked behind the plate for 10 years, averaging 70.6 games per year, and in 1,970 at bats hit safely 506 times with 67 doubles, 14 triples, and six homers (dead-ball era), batting .257 and slugging .314. He also scored 196 runs and drove in 235.

Rough Carrigan took over the team in the middle of the 1913 season from Jake Stahl, who had won the pennant the year before. Stahl was having a losing season (39–41), and the front office decided to make a change. Carrigan took over and finished the season by winning 40 of the last 70 games. Getting the team back to its winning ways, Carrigan guided the club to a second-place finish in 1914, with 91 wins and 62 losses. Thus he set the stage for his two winning seasons in 1915 and 1916.

Joe Cronin was yet another player-manager of the Red Sox. He was a player-manager for 11 of the 13 years he guided the club. Cronin was not as fortunate as Collins and Carrigan, but he did win the pennant in 1946 after the team had finished seventh the year before. Cronin's teams were almost always competitive, and four times they finished second.

As a player Joe Cronin was one of the few shortstops who retired with an above-.300 batting average. As a result he earned a birth in the Hall of Fame in 1956. He collected 2,285 hits, which included 515 doubles, 118 triples, and 170 home runs.

The hard-hitting shortstop led the league in doubles in 1933 and 1938, in triples in 1932, and in pinch hits toward the end of his career in 1943. He came to the Red Sox in a trade from the Washington Senators, who received shortstop Lynn Lary, who possessed a lifetime batting average of .267 and a fine glove. In addition the Red Sox, who were extremely high on Cronin, paid $225,000 in cash. This was a huge sum of money in 1935 and is interesting because just 15 years earlier the club received only $125,000 from the Yankees for Babe Ruth. Inflation was hardly in existence in those days, and it was amazing that Boston would pay almost twice as much for Cronin as they received for Ruth. The club's desire for Cronin was a result of his hitting over .300 4 years in a row for the Senators. Cronin did not disappoint the front office, as he hit over .300 six times in the 10 years he was active. He had a high of .325 in 1938. While with the Senators his best effort was a .346 in 1930.

Joe Cronin was a fine fielding shortstop who led the league 16 times in various fielding categories.

BIBLIOGRAPHY

Murray, Tom
SPORT Magazine's All-Time All-Stars
New York: Atheneum, 1977

Reichler, Joseph L., ed.
The Baseball Encyclopedia:
The Complete & Official Record of Major League Baseball
New York: Macmillan, 1987

Seymour, Harold
Baseball: The Early Years
Toronto: Oxford University Press, 1960

Carter, Craig, ed.
The Complete Baseball Record Book
St. Louis, Missouri: The Sporting News, 1987

Siwoff, Seymour
The Book of Baseball Records
New York: Sterling, 1981

Smith, Robert
The Pioneers of Baseball
Boston: Little, Brown & Co., 1978

Turkin, Hy, and S. C. Thompson
The Official Encyclopedia of Baseball, 10th edition
South Brunswick, N.J.: A. S. Barnes, 1979